Tom Cox is the author of several bestselling books, including two previous memoirs about his adventures in cat ownership: *Under the Paw* and *Talk to the Tail*. He is on Twitter at @cox_tom and blogs at www.littlecatdiaries. blogspot.co.uk

Also by this author

Under the Paw
Talk to the Tail

The Good, The Bad And The Furry

Life With The World's Most Melancholy Cat And Other Whiskery Friends

TOM COX

SPHERE

First published in Great Britain in 2013 by Sphere

11 13 15 17 19 20 18 16 14 12

Copyright © Tom Cox 2013

The moral right of the author has been asserted.

All rights reserved.
No part of this publication may be reproduced, stored in a
retrieval system, or transmitted, in any form or by any means, without
the prior permission in writing of the publisher, nor be otherwise circulated
in any form of binding or cover other than that in which it is published
and without a similar condition including this condition being
imposed on the subsequent purchaser.

A CIP catalogue record for this book
is available from the British Library.

ISBN 978-0-7515-5239-3

Typeset in Goudy by M Rules
Printed and bound in Great Britain by
Clays Ltd, St Ives plc

Papers used by Sphere are from well-managed forests
and other responsible sources.

MIX
Paper from
responsible sources
FSC® C104740

Sphere
An imprint of
Little, Brown Book Group
100 Victoria Embankment
London EC4Y 0DY

An Hachette UK Company
www.hachette.co.uk

www.littlebrown.co.uk

For Jo and Mick

'He absorbed that something in the demeanours of Bears reminds us of ourselves. They have the faces of outcasts.'

Rose Tremain, *Merivel*

CATPACITY

For a human to reach the absolute limit of cats a person can reasonably own without doing serious damage to his or her own mental state, or that of the cats. E.g.: 'Man, I would love to take that kitten off your hands, believe me, but I'm totally at catpacity right now.'

CATPAWCITY

The exact opposite of being at catpacity: a state of cat-lessness, leading to an unenriched life. Not to be confused with the nineteenth-century American frontier town, Cat Paw City, North Dakota (population 301).

Reynardine

My cat Janet had been sick outside my back door. Or, as it might have seemed to you, had you never met Janet before and arrived upon the scene as an innocent: a large tanker of vomit had swerved off the road and into my garden, shedding its entire load in the process, and now my cat Janet was inspecting its contents. I knew better than that. Ever since he'd first bounded clumsily into my life a decade earlier, Janet – who was actually a large man cat – had been a master puker, a veritable titan of regurgitation. It had nothing to do with the fact that he'd been ill for the last couple of years. He'd always been the same. Sometimes, sitting several feet away, I'd spot him apparently beginning to re-enact the moves from the video for the 1997 remix of Run DMC's 'It's Like That' single; then I'd be able to rush over in time to thrust a used broadsheet newspaper or cardboard box in front of his face and avert disaster. But a person couldn't reasonably be expected to be on vomit stakeout 24/7.

At least on this occasion he'd been considerate enough to puke outdoors.

'You don't need to clean that up,' said my friend Mary, gesturing towards Janet and his vomit. She and her boyfriend Will had been staying at my house the night before and, like me, had been woken up by another of my cats, Ralph, meowing his own name at 5 a.m. 'Give it a couple of days and a fox will be along to eat it all.'

'Really?' I asked. 'Are you sure?'

'Definitely. Foxes always eat my mum's dog's vomit. They love it.'

'It's true,' said Will, nod-wincing in a manner that simultaneously managed to convey both his faith in Mary's opinion and his distaste for the eating of vomit.

'RAAAAAALPH,' said Ralph, who, despite our previous speculation to the contrary, evidently hadn't quite finished his daily morning session of meowing his own name.

I have a lot of friends who love animals, but none are more knowledgeable than Will and Mary. The first time I met them, at a used record fair, they told me they'd spent a considerable part of the previous afternoon watching a wasp eat a bench. This pretty much set the tone for our friendship, which revolves roughly half around enthusing about early 1970s Greek progressive rock and half around looking at photos of owls and hares and saying, 'Yep. That's a good one.' If I'm out in the countryside, I'm fairly unconditional in my mission to befriend any creature with four legs or some kind of fur or feathers on it, but I don't have any of the facts at my fingertips. Will and Mary are different. If I plan a country walk with them, I need to allow an extra forty-two per cent on top of its usual duration just for the time they spend pointing out rare fungi and birdlife. This is great for me, as I get my usual fresh air and exercise buzz, plus the chance to learn lots of new things – yesterday, for example, on an icy walk through the north-western edge of Thetford Forest, I'd found out what a woodcock was by seeing Mary walk up to a woodcock and say, 'Look! It's a fucking woodcock!'

Will and Mary were representative of what had turned out, to nobody's greater surprise than my own, to be a good year for me. Eighteen months previously, in the spring of 2009, I'd broken up with my partner of almost nine years. A couple of weeks after that a friend had died very suddenly of an undetected brain tumour and I'd been given the news that my nan – my lone remaining grandparent, who'd always been almost like a second mum to me – had terminal lung cancer. I'd found myself alone, in a house far too big for me where everything seemed to be falling to bits, with four of the six cats my ex, Dee, and I had owned, in a county – Norfolk – where none of my family lived and where, it began to occur to me, I hadn't tried quite as hard as I might to make new friends.

Dee and I had decided on a one-third to two-thirds split of our six cats. This had been solely based on what would be best for the cats themselves, in terms of environment and stress levels. To put it another way, she had taken with her the two young cats who loved each other, while I'd got the four old grumpy ones, each of whom thought the others were giant buttmunches. There was Ralph, a preening tabby who liked to meow his own name outside my bedroom window at 5 a.m., lived in constant terror of my metal clothes horse, took umbrage at cleanly washed hands, and had a habit of bringing slugs into the house on his back. There was his strong, wiry brother Shipley, who stole soup and was constantly mouthing off at everyone, but generally relaxed once you picked him up and turned him upside down. Then there was Janet, who was clumsy, often accidentally set fire to his tail by walking too close to lighted candles, liked bringing old crisp packets into the house, and suffered from a weak heart and an overactive thyroid gland, dictating that I had to find stealthy ways to make him swallow two small pink pills every day to keep him alive.

Finally, there was The Bear. Now well past his fifteenth birthday, he was a troubled gothic poet of a cat with a penchant for pissing on the bedroom curtains and a meow redolent of the ghost of an eighteenth-century animal – I tended to change my mind as to precisely which *kind* of eighteenth-century animal. Like Janet, The Bear had been Dee's cat from a previous relationship. More than that, he had the stigma of being her previous ex's favourite cat. Despite this, we had both agreed that, between Dee and me, he liked me most. There were various undeniable signs of this: for example, he enjoyed getting on my lap and looking deep into my eyes whilst purring, and he had never snuck into a basket of clean laundry and neatly deposited a turd inside the pocket of my dressing gown, or pissed on one of my legs during one of our arguments.

All of these cats had led me, in the months immediately following our split, inexorably back into a long-defunct relationship. Their stories were mine and Dee's; their numerous nicknames would, I worried, sound wrong if I said them in the house the two of us had shared, in the presence of someone who wasn't her. They were the four closest, most painful points on a personal map of Norfolk called 'Us' which, whether I liked it or not, had come to define my first, somewhat lost, summer as a single person.

But then something unexpected had happened: I'd begun to feel quite good. Better, and more free, and more *me*, than I'd felt for years. Instead of scurrying away to see old friends who lived in other parts of the country, as I had been doing previously, I began making an effort to meet people close by, and found it amazingly easy. I got to know and fall in love with Norfolk like never before. I ate an apple every day, abandoned the vitamin tablets I used to take, and went on at least one long country walk every week. Before I knew it, I'd gone the first year of my adult life without getting a cold. I was fitter and slimmer at thirty-five than I'd been since I was twenty. If I had any worries that all this had turned me into a big girly post-divorce spiritual empowerment living-in-the-moment cliché, the simple fact of my increased happiness suffocated them.

My life now, a year and a half on from the break-up,

was one mostly comprised of good friends, dancing, abuse from my cats, hamfisted attempts at DIY, diminishing amounts of TV, and lots of fresh air. I definitely didn't view my cats as children, but my relationship with my house had become like that of a single parent and a giant, adored problem child with decaying limbs and windows for a face. It was the first building of my own I'd ever loved – a somewhat brutal early sixties structure known as the Upside Down House, whose kitchen was found on the top one of its three floors – but a new bit of it seemed to break every week. The days when I could afford to buy nice new furniture for it or keep it looking tiptop seemed long, long in the past, but I found that I didn't miss them – wondered, even, if any of that had really been so important to me. My cats were happy and safe, while I had a warm, dry place to sleep and a quiet place to work and read; these seemed like the most important things.

I was also still high on the amazing, dizzying sense of possibility that came with waking up each day as a single person. But I was aware that that was a novelty with a limited lifespan, and that, as much happiness as I had, it was the kind that came with its own empty compartment. Until last year, I'd been in long-term relationships pretty much all my adult life and it still seemed, to me, like a natural state for a person to be in. I would, despite everything, very much like to be in one again. At least, that's what I kept telling myself.

'So,' said Mary. 'You haven't told us how it went last week.'

'It was OK,' I said. 'No, good. Really nice.'

'So are you going to see her again?'

'Maybe. But probably just as friends.'

'Dude,' said Will. 'You are one of the pickiest guys I know.'

'I know,' I said. 'I'm a nightmare.'

'RAAAAALPH,' said Ralph.

Over the course of the last fourteen months, I'd found no shortage of people wanting to set me up on dates, but little had come of any of those that I'd been on. The problem, more often than not, was my own state of mind. Beth, who I'd caught the train down to London to see the previous Friday, was a case in point. A funny, bookish, curvaceous, dark-haired animal lover who liked 1970s classic rock, she was about as right for me on paper as anyone could possibly be. A couple of weeks earlier, we'd spent a perfectly lovely afternoon by the river in Norwich, followed by a gig at the Arts Centre. 'There's something I have to warn you about, if you're going to date me,' she had told me during the second half of the evening.

I braced myself for the inevitable baggage. I was in my thirties now, and could take this. Did she have seven children with eight different dads? Had she been a contestant on a reality TV show?

'My cat, Neil, is a bit of a liability,' she said.

'Oh, really?' I said. I felt pretty calm. I'd met a lot of liability cats in my time.

'Yep. He's bad. The other day I was sitting in the front room with my flatmate and my flatmate's girlfriend, and

Neil walked into the room and seemed to be choking on something. I rushed over to him and pulled it out of his mouth. It turned out to be my flatmate's used condom. I ended up with quite a lot of the ... stuff in it on my hands.'

Admittedly, this was pretty extreme, but, in truth, Neil's behaviour didn't worry me – not even when, on our second date, Beth told me of an unfortunate incident involving a sexual encounter, a sudden, unexpected appearance from Neil, and a very intimate part of her last boyfriend's anatomy. I knew Beth was great, and that in theory I was a fool for not wanting to take things further with her. Had she been three times as bright and attractive and lived with a cat who *didn't* have a penchant for eating used condoms and clawing men's testicles, I probably still would have come away from our dates with the same shrugging outlook; the outlook of someone who'd only split up from the most important and lengthy relationship of his life a year and a bit ago and, despite his attempts to tell himself otherwise, wasn't yet in any frame of mind to be heading into another serious one.

If anything, I'd gone out of my way *not* to go out with women with an extreme love of cats – partly because it's my habit to insist on doing everything in life in the most difficult manner possible, and partly because I'd been put off by a few slightly invasive incidents involving the unhinged 0.5 per cent of cat enthusiasts who give the 99.5 per cent of stable and lovely ones a bad name. I also couldn't quite escape the lingering knowledge that in the past, with the exception of Dee, I'd seemingly been attracted solely to women who either actively disliked cats or were allergic to them. That had been a long time ago, and I could write it off as sheer coincidence, but a few of my early experiences as a single thirtysomething suggested otherwise. The following conversation, for example, that I had with a pretty Irish girl from a TV production company, who I got chatting to after she did a vox pop with my friend during a lull between bands at the 2010 Latitude Festival in Suffolk:

Me: 'Who've you been to see so far this weekend?'

Pretty Irish girl: 'Black Mountain. They were the best.'

Me: 'Me too. I loved them! I've been to see them three times this year.'

Pretty Irish Girl: 'Me too! No, sorry, four! I love that seventies stoner rock stuff. I like your trousers, by the way. So what do you do for a living?'

Me: 'I write books and a couple of newspaper columns.'

Pretty Irish girl: 'Oh, really? Cool. What kind of books?'

Me: 'Well, a few different kinds. The last couple were mainly about cats, though.'

Pretty Irish girl: 'Cats?'

Me: 'Yeah. And two about golf.'

Pretty Irish girl: 'Golf? Oh. Weird. I hate cats. They're all evil.'

Who was I trying to fool? *Of course* I couldn't expect to share my life happily with someone who actively disliked cats, or even grumblingly tolerated them. I'd met a few unusually delightful anti-cat folk, but people who hated cats were often control freaks who felt the world owed them a living. People who expected other people to be eager and compliant, no matter how poorly they treated them. Churchill and Roosevelt loved cats. Hitler and Napoleon hated them. That was a vastly reductive view of the matter, obviously, but it told you a lot. How could I look someone in the eye if they told me they didn't like The Bear? Even Katia, my former lodger, a dyed-in-the-wool Dog Person, had loved The Bear. 'Ralph is the guy I fancy, but The Bear is the guy I love,' she said, not long before she moved out. 'The other two are cats.'

I drove Will and Mary to the railway station a couple of miles away and we said goodbye. When I got back to the house, Shipley was upside down on a beanbag that had, before it became permanently flecked with his hair, once been mine. Janet was on the floor to the left of him, breathing quite heavily, as he often did these days. I decided not to attempt to stroke him or ruffle his scruff, as I knew he probably still hadn't forgiven me for medicating him earlier. The process had taken the best part of twenty minutes and, though I'd wrapped the pills cunningly in some turkey roll, had entailed one of them getting spat out and stuck variously to my trouser leg, a chair and two of the other cats' backs. The Bear was outside on what, when I bought the house, had been described in the estate agent's details as a 'balcony', but in recent years had come to serve more as a kind of roofless, assisted-living flat of The Bear's very own.

As I sat down on the sofa with a book, Ralph appeared. I didn't have the metal clothes horse out that day, and hadn't washed my hands in the last hour, so he was in a good mood. 'RAAAALPH! RAaalph!' he shouted, jumping on top of me and beginning to pad my chest. He didn't actually stick a flag into it emblazoned with the words 'Cats rule!' but we both knew the intention was there.

Happiness becomes a much more complex thing to weigh when you get older. Even if it's quite bulky overall, it tends to have little rips and chasms in it. Sometimes a wave of sadness will wash over a chasm and remind you of its presence. For me, one of these chasms was about not having someone to share these cats with, and at times like now, when I was at home alone, shortly after spending time with friends, I'd often sense its presence. Four cats, after all, seemed quite a lot for one person – significantly more than six shared between two people had seemed. Katia had got it spot on. Living with my cats often seemed less like living with four cats and more like living with two cats plus a glamorous, oversensitive rock star and a troubled yet loyal elderly academic, both of whom just happened to be a foot high and covered in fur. The Bear broke my heart on an hourly basis with his big watery eyes and his tiny *meoop*: a much gentler noise than a normal meow, but one that could still pull noisily at your heartstrings with its central question, which seemed to translate roughly as 'Can you tell me why I am a cat, please?' I'd bought him a catnip rat and some turkey chunks for (what I decided must roughly be the date of) his last birthday, but it had somehow seemed insufficient. I sensed, deep down, that he might have preferred the latest Jonathan Franzen novel, or a new Werner Herzog documentary that I'd been hearing very good things about.

I could think of few revelations about my day-to-day life that would have made me feel more unmoored than if someone had found a way to measure cat IQs and discovered as a result that The Bear was a simpleton. I'd been acquainted with this cat for well over a decade now, and I felt I knew his intellectual powers. Even if those soulful peepers signified nothing and mere coincidence explained his disappearances in the build-up to every house move I'd ever made, or his eerie way of gravitating towards me every time I was ill or sad, you could not doubt that he had had the most character-building of cat lives: all nine of the standard allocation, plus seven or eight bonus ones he seemed to have been granted as a special favour.

The Bear and Ralph could not have been more different, in terms of facial expressions. The Bear went about with a permanent look of saucer-eyed worry. He'd originally been found in a plastic bag on the hard shoulder of a motorway, along with several of his siblings. In his youth his fur had all fallen out due to a flea allergy, then fallen out again due to an allergy to flea treatment medicine. He'd withstood carbon monoxide poisoning, had a hole ripped in his throat by a feral challenger, developed asthma, lost chunks of both ears, gone AWOL for almost six weeks in south London, moved house over a dozen times, and been rather brutally given his marching orders on countless occasions by Biscuit, my next door neighbours' cat, whose *Last of the Summer Wine* affection he pined for. To look at The Bear was to see the worry of all that with the worry of the rest of the world piled on top of it. If the eyes are the windows to a cat's soul, The Bear's made those of all other cats look like they were made of tinted glass.

A few months ago, I'd had my house valued by a few estate agents, in order that Dee and I could agree on a price for me to buy her out of the mortgage. Having gone off to make one of the estate agents a cup of tea, I returned to the living room to find him and The Bear staring at each other, intensely, like two old adversaries who had not seen each other since the time many years ago when one stole the other's dream job and childhood sweetheart.

'Wow. Who is this?' asked the estate agent.

'That's The Bear,' I said.

'He's amazing. It's like there's a little bloke inside there.'

'I know. A lot of people say that.'

The Bear did not blithely let the universe revolve around him, like many cats. He examined each molecule of it intently and anxiously.

Ralph, by contrast, was a cat who beamed with self-satisfaction on a near-permanent basis: an animal so pleased with himself that he walked around every morning talking about himself in the third person. But they were both needy: cats who were nervous around strangers

and seemed to want something from me that, no matter how much I wanted to, I could not quite pinpoint, much less give them. Ralph wasn't the kind of cat who could be content with being next to you. When he climbed on my chest, he expected no half measures. He wanted my undivided attention and worship. In one sense, this was fine: he was arguably the most majestic of my cats.

People were always telling me how handsome he was, and he had a way of making it feel like he was granting you a rare pleasure when he let you stroke his magnificent sideburns. But the experience came with its own inherent risks. A bit like Jim Morrison at the height of The Doors' fame, he was a paradoxical combination of beauty and questionable personal hygiene. He was the kind of cat who, were he left to fend for himself, would probably be followed everywhere by a squad of opportunistic flies, in much the same way that seagulls follow ships.

Maybe it was a measure of their very worship of an animal who was essentially a cross between a lion and a young Warren Beatty, but smaller creatures had a way of attaching themselves to Ralph. A recent example were the slugs that had infested my kitchen. I don't really associate slugs with the height of winter, but throughout December a multi-coloured tag team of them had snuck in through one of the increasingly large holes in the walls and began making their presence felt. At first, I'd seen a couple wriggling about in the cat biscuit dispenser, like nightmarish limbless children playing in an unusually grimy ballpit. Then, a week or so later, I noticed a strange, brown, elongated raspberry in a bowl of Country Crisp I'd just poured out from a box that had been left untouched for a fortnight or so. I then noticed, somewhat more perturbingly, that it was moving. Pretty soon, perhaps having checked out my other cats and found them substandard hosts, the slugs began attaching themselves to Ralph's back. This could come as a nasty shock, on the occasions when I was sprawled out on the sofa, watching TV with Ralph sitting smugly on top of me. I did, though, find that the upset was reduced slightly if I imagined that I was actually looking at a snake riding a small horse.

Janet (so named because Dee had been erroneously told he was a she, by the East End urchins from whom she adopted him) was my number two most unkempt and unhygienic cat – or my number one, if you were to go with Katia's theory that Ralph and The Bear weren't cats at all. For the last couple of years, he'd been bringing in all manner of ancient sweet wrappers and crisp packets that he'd found floating in the shallows of the lake at the bottom of my garden. He could often be found with a collection of twigs, or a considerable part of the fresh undercoat from one of my neighbours' garden gates, stuck to his hindquarters. His dishevelled appearance wasn't really his own fault, though. He'd been a large, muscular cat in his youth, but when his hyperthyroidism had been at its worst, the spring before last, in the midst of my break-up with Dee, he'd lost so much weight that he'd started to resemble a recently used black dust cloth. With the upping of his medication, he'd gained some weight and seemed happier, but he wasn't the happy-go-lucky cat he used to be. Never was this more clearly illustrated than in the wrestling bouts that Shipley still attempted to involve him in. Theirs was the nearest thing any two of my cats had to a friendship: a bit like a big brother–little brother bond in which the little brother was having trouble accepting that the big brother would probably rather now be going on a cruise or watching repeats of *Murder She Wrote* than rolling around on the floor in a bundle of limbs.

As my two 'cat' cats, Shipley and Janet were also the most public, my 'people cats' – although in Shipley's case I suspect this was largely because it's very hard to subjugate and intimidate people when you're not around them. They were always the first – and often the only – cats to greet my visitors: when my hippie folk musician friend Michael visited a couple of weeks after Will and Mary, Shipley was at him with a volley of questions almost as soon as he was through the door. This was a lot to take in for Michael, who moves at a pace that is very much his own, but thankfully Shipley soon calmed down, settling into a bout of passionate lovemaking with the velvet cape Michael had taken off and made the mistake of leaving unattended on a sofa.

There were those – Dee being amongst them – who'd suggested in the past that what Shipley really needed was the cat version of Borstal, or at least National Service, but I preferred to believe that he was misunderstood. Following me around and profanely assassinating my character was just his way of telling me he needed love. All anyone had to do was pick him up and turn him upside down and he was putty in their hands. This was a view shared by my neighbour, Deborah, who adored him.

'Shipley came over again this morning,' she would tell me. 'He used some pretty awful language and had some very hurtful things to say to me, but we had a cuddle anyway. He seemed OK after that.'

It was fine for Deborah, her husband David, and me: we were humans, and knew how to turn Shipley from a grade-one gobshite into a purring lovebundle in ten seconds flat. If you were a fellow feline, though, especially one of a quiet or geriatric disposition, and didn't have the physical capability to turn him upside down, having him constantly in your face talking trash must have been quite tiresome. Ralph, who was so strong he probably *could* have turned him upside down if he'd really wanted to, suffered his tomfoolery, but when the avalanche of attitude got too much would assert his dominance by calmly bashing Shipley's head against the nearest hard surface. The Bear, who abhorred all straightforward forms of violence, did his best to keep out of his way. Janet had once welcomed his advances, in a boisterous way, but now would often slink irritably away into a quiet corner.

Snow arrived the following month, which was a shame, because, for the previous few weeks, taking Mary's advice, I'd been deliberately neglecting to clear up the sick Janet had deposited outside the back door. This had resulted in a bet with Mary and Will: my £10 said that some remnant of the sick would still be there at Easter. I was genuinely intrigued to know how long a heap of sick could survive on its own in the wild. My initial reason for leaving the sick, however, had been my desire to meet a fox, then to possibly become friends with it, learning to take the good with the bad and to overlook the flaws in its personality, such as, say, the fact that it liked to eat other animals' puke.

It had been a while since I'd had a regular local fox. You had to go back a full decade, when Janet had befriended one in the communal garden of my old flat in south-east London. This was a truly sorry-looking creature, about as near as a real fox could come to looking like an empty fox costume that had been left in a gutter, but Janet would sit happily alongside it on the lawn for long periods, simply watching the day go by. To me this always seemed an impressively non-ageist gesture from a cat who was in the prime of life and could easily have won the respect of far more robust, up-and-coming alpha animals, if he'd wanted to.

These days Janet had a lot more in common with that old fox, who had no doubt long since trotted off to the great den in the sky. I still sometimes heard Janet outside, nobly defending the house from intruder cats, but his spine felt weak when I stroked it and he was far more skittish than he'd ever been, especially at mealtimes. Sometimes he'd hang back and not eat at all. I wished I could have explained to him somehow that I was giving him the pills for his own good. Towards the close of 2010, 'I give you these because I love you and I don't want you to die' was probably top of the list of sentences I would have liked to be able to translate into felinese for my cats – above even such other classics as 'Please stop hurting me with your eyes' and 'It's a carrot. You wouldn't like it.'

Janet had always seemed less keen than The Bear, Ralph or Shipley to impress his eccentricities and hang-ups on me: if it is possible for a cat to be angst-ridden – and I think it is – that was a trait he'd been spared. When you compared him to The Bear, though, what you saw was the cat world reversing all the clichés you'd ever heard about worry acting as an ageing device. At thirteen, Janet was the younger of the pair by three years, but The Bear, who'd looked not unlike a wizened Gremlin when I'd first known him, now appeared far more youthful.

'How old do you reckon he is? Go on, have a guess!' I'd encourage people who were meeting The Bear for the first time.

'Five?' they'd say, more often than not. 'Six? Definitely not more than eight.'

I had to face facts, though: I lived with two elderly cats, and two others who were well into middle age. At the end of January, I took the second oldest for his regular blood test at the vet's. The new vet, who had a strong Swedish accent – all the vets who'd ever looked after my cats seemed to have strong regional accents – said Janet had lost a little weight but that it was probably nothing to worry about. As I drove home from the surgery, the rain bucketed down and washed the snow off the streets. By that afternoon, the last remaining slush had gone from the path near the back door, but, amazingly, the vomit was still there. Except now it had a green tint around its edges that seemed to be oozing outwards, and a cat – probably Shipley or Ralph, the resident mousers – had left a couple of rodent corpses next to it. These foxes were really missing out on a treat now. Where on earth were they?

Since becoming a single person with these cats, I found that my life could be viewed from two different angles. From Angle One, I was still young(ish), with none of the financial or emotional trauma of children from a previous relationship, had a nice house of my own, in a very beautiful part of the country, and a job I loved (I COULD DO ANYTHING!). Then there was Angle Two: I had little money, having bought my partner out of a mortgage, the two industries in which I earned a living – publishing and journalism – were in crisis, and I spent a lot of my days cleaning up small dead animals and looking after a bigger, poorly one, whose condition severely limited how long I could spend away from home (I COULDN'T REALLY DO THAT MUCH, IF I WAS COMPLETELY HONEST!).

In the three months that the sick had been present I'd swung from being a breezy member of the Angle One camp significantly towards the Angle Two school of thought. The rural winter had begun with an enchanting kind of darkness, but now the weeks had begun to drag and it felt more engulfing. My dad – who'd broken his spine thirteen months previously – was unwell. It was starting to feel like such a gargantuan aeon since I'd been in love that I wondered if it would ever happen again. I'd never had more friends who were ill or out of work. And, to compound all this, in early February, while DJing at a bar in Norwich, I'd burned a sizeable chunk of my hair off by setting fire to it on a tealight candle.

It's a difficult one, setting fire to your own hair by accident. First of all there's the fact that you lose some of your hair, but there's also the fact that, if you're in company while it happens, you have to put on a brave face and be kind of jovial about it. I'd laughed in front of strangers and friends as, bending down to find the groove marking the beginning of 'We're An American Band' on a Grand Funk Railroad album, in a booth illuminated only by that tealight, I'd begun first to sizzle and then to slap my own head furiously to put out the blaze. I'd continued to chuckle and joke about it for the next hour, as I wandered around with my own brand new signature smell. But, later, when I examined the damage in the mirror, I was horrified to find a considerable portion of the hair on the front of my head gone. I began to regret all those times I'd laughed at Janet for catching his tail on a candle or joss stick.

It was with this in mind, as well as a general mission to make him more comfortable and happy at mealtimes, that I headed to the pet shop down the road the following day and bought him some Applaws – a cat food so upmarket it's slightly surprising that it doesn't come with its own croutons and miniature bag of parmesan. He wolfed this down enthusiastically, then sat beside me on the sofa, purring loudly, though if pushed I would probably say he was purring more at me than with me: his way of saying, 'Now, see: how do *you* like it?'

The day after that, I got up late, having travelled down to London and back in the evening. For the journey I'd worn a smart, wide-brimmed hat, which covered my frazzled patch. A couple of friends had complimented me on the hat, but I'd also seen a small child in my train carriage look across at me then ask her mum a question about a circus. If I was being honest, I had my doubts about whether it was a look I'd stick to on a permanent basis.

As I emerged from the bathroom, wincing as I caught sight of my frazzled patch in the mirror, I heard a loud, wrenching sound from a couple of rooms away. I would compare it to the sound of a long-unoiled door being ripped from its hinges, yet it was too animal and visceral for that.

I hurried into the living room and saw Shipley standing up, alert, looking in the direction of the staircase that led to the lower floor of the house. I think, even then, that I knew, because I approached the stairs in a wide, cautious circle. To a bystander it probably would have looked like I was preparing for the world's most apprehensive high jump. My thoughts weren't clear or ordered, but perhaps there was a part of my brain that wondered if the noise had come from a creature brought in by the cats. Shipley had clearly been sleeping before he heard it, though, and Ralph, the other homicidal maniac, remained fast asleep on the top floor. I turned the corner onto the stairs and found Janet slumped awkwardly across two of them.

He looked deflated, like a furry cat balloon, and as I

ran to him and held him I saw the last glimmer of life fade from his eyes. A small trickle of blood seeped from his mouth onto the stair, and I gently lifted his paw, asking myself if he could be in some kind of temporary paralysis, but I knew – even though I'd never previously been with anyone, pet or human, at the moment of death – that he'd gone. He had suffered a heart attack, and the best thing I could say about it was that he clearly did not have to endure for long whatever terrible pain had wrenched that noise from him.

The summer before last, when Dee and I had been dividing our possessions, I'd had a recurring nightmare in which I buried an old black cat, unaccompanied, in the rain. I'd told her about the nightmare, and she'd assured me that it was something I'd never have to do. Janet had been Dee's cat long before she'd known me, so, having wrapped his body in a blanket, the first thing I did was call her. But there was no answer. I left her a tearful voicemail, explaining what had happened to Janet.

As it turned out, she did not reply until that evening. When she did, with a voicemail of her own – I was driving at the time, on my way to meet Katia and our friend Jamie, who had offered to buy me a consoling drink – I was surprised that her message, while sympathetic, did not sound more upset, or particularly inviting of a return call. But I rationalised the situation. During our first few months apart, I'd missed our other two cats, Pablo and Bootsy, terribly. Every time I saw the cover of the hardback edition of the first book I'd written about my cats, they were there, staring adorably and wonkily out at me, but they were far away, and it was highly likely I'd never see them again. To mentally remove myself from them had been a matter of survival. I'm sure Dee had done the same with the other four. She lived more than a hundred miles away now, and our existences had become entirely separate.

When my second childhood cat, Tabs, was run over, in 1986, my dad had sprung into action and protected me, making sure I was locked inside the house as he took her body from the side of the road and buried her in the garden. In a way, when one of our animals dies in a vet's surgery, the vet performs a minor version of the role my dad played that day: they're parents, for just a few minutes. But when a cat dies at home, we're alone – even more so when we live on our own, and none of our closest friends are within twenty miles of us. I can honestly say that in the next two hours I felt more isolated than I had in my entire life. I wondered about going over to see Deborah and David next door, who'd both loved Janet and had even recently shot a home video of him on their decking, running away from a pheasant. But they would probably both be at work. 'Should I call the vet?' I'd wondered when I found Janet. 'No,' I chided myself. 'That would be ridiculous.' What did I expect them to do? My local surgery didn't have paramedics, or its own ambulance. I called my lovely mum, who was

terrific and calmed me down, even though, being several counties away, she probably felt a bit helpless
herself.

I carried Janet across the lawn – his weight, more than
restored, in death, to what it had been in the prime of his
life, came as a shock – and buried him under the apple
tree at the bottom of the garden. It was one whose
branches he and Shipley used to like to race up and
down in pursuit of one another. In my tear- and rain-
stained grief, I still found a second or two to wonder if a
previous owner of the house had ever buried a pet here
before, and thought of a story my friend Jackie had told
me about her cat Martha, who'd died the previous year.
While burying Martha, in similarly sodden conditions,
on the hillside where she lived in Pembrokeshire, poor
Jackie had accidentally dug up the skeleton of Martha's
brother, Arthur, who'd died seven years earlier after
being hit by a car. 'I must have looked a right state,' she
told me, 'standing in the rain, covered in mud, bawling
my eyes out, holding the corpse of one cat and the skeleton of another. It's a good job nobody was walking along
the footpath at the time.' I thought with horror and sym-
pathy about the people out there who are *truly* alone
when an animal dies – who, unlike Jackie and me, don't
have the comfort of loving family, or the knowledge that,
even though they live a bit out of the way, before long
they'll see friends who'll help them feel better.

So: my cat had died, it was raining, and I was moment-
arily isolated, but part of me still knew it could be worse.
'It could be worse': I couldn't remember having said that

very much in my first twenty-five years on the planet, but it is so often the reassuring mantra of adulthood. And what I was experiencing now really was adulthood, in a more extreme way than I'd ever experienced it.

People have a lot of different definitions of what makes you a proper grown-up. Some claim it's getting your first car or losing your virginity. Others think it's buying your first house or having your first child. For me, it was the moment when alone, in the pouring rain, far from nearly all of the people I loved, I buried my cat, twenty minutes after holding him in my arms and watching him die.

As I tramped back up the steep garden towards the house, I saw The Bear staring down at me from the living-room window. With his huge saucer eyes and the rain running down the glass, you could have set the scene to music as the climactic montage in a heart-breaking Hollywood movie. If you'd never met him before, you'd have been sure he was in mourning. But The Bear always looked like that. He was the only cat I'd ever seen who appeared to be almost permanently on the verge of tears. He'd never exactly disliked Janet, but had suffered him as the painfully intelligent have always suffered the trivial and frivolous. Would he be sad without him? Perhaps. But in his deep, mysterious, faintly omniscient way, I imagine he probably had known it was coming.

I arrived inside and sat beside him. I was struck, as so often, by how well he had aged. His ears looked a bit like they'd been nibbled by a large rabbit who'd mistaken them for a couple of small black lettuce leaves, but, even if his eyes were impossibly sad, they were bright too, and his fur was much shinier than it had been when I'd first met him. I picked him up and he clung tightly to me, as if holding on for dear life. Again, probably nothing to do with the circumstances of the moment. The Bear always clung tightly to the chests of those he liked as if holding on for dear life. 'Wow, man,' Michael the folk musician with the cape, who'd looked after him for a while, had once said. 'That was intense when I first cuddled him. I don't think I've ever felt anything like that from a cat before.' That was a decade and a marriage ago, but I still felt the same thing, every day.

'Just the four of us now, then,' I said, and he began to purr.

The following day, after an evening spent with my supportive friends in Norwich, I noticed something odd: the sick outside the back door was gone, leaving no trace of its long and clinging tenancy. Mary and Will would be pleased and vindicated to find out. Had it already vanished yesterday? I couldn't say, as I'd been too fogged by grief to notice. You could say the rain was probably responsible, but there had been heavy downpours several times during the last few weeks and they hadn't succeeded in shifting it. To me it all seemed a bit suspicious. One day, I've got a load of vomit outside my back door and no willing, hungry foxes in the neighbourhood. The next day, my cat, who once happened to be best friends with a very thin, old fox, badly in need of sustenance, dies. The day after that, I've got absolutely no vomit outside my back door.

Alongside the one that involved me telling myself that Janet did not suffer for long, it became one of the positive thoughts I tried to focus on, in the days that followed: maybe he had finally been reunited with his old (not all that) bushy-tailed friend from London? I pictured the scene: Janet's immortal soul leaving his body, climbing into the apple tree and spotting the fox's immortal soul trotting across the lawn.

'You certainly took your time,' says the fox's immortal soul.

'I was busy. What can I say? We moved house a lot. There was a break-up to deal with. Life gets in the way, you know,' says Janet's immortal soul.

'I just found some really tasty vomit by the door, on my way here,' says the fox's immortal soul.

'That came from me!' says Janet's immortal soul.

'Ooh, thanks! Very good of you,' says the fox's immortal soul. 'There were a couple of voles, too, but they were a bit wet and chewy, and one was technically just a vole's bottom.'

'Yeah,' says Janet's immortal soul. 'Shipley likes to eat their faces. Don't ask me why. He's a massive weirdo.'

'Anyway, let's not hang around,' says the fox's immortal soul. 'I've got lots to show you.'

'Great!' says Janet's immortal soul. 'I'm excited.'

'Just watch you don't set fire to your tail when you

pass through the fiery vortex separating this dimension from the next,' says the fox's immortal soul. 'I did that in 2002 and the fur I lost took ages to grow back.'

'Gotcha,' says Janet's immortal soul.

Just before they leave, Janet's immortal soul pauses. It has a worried look on its face. 'Shit!'

'What's wrong?' asks the fox's immortal soul.

'You just cost him a tenner.'

The Ten Catmandments

Thou shalt have no other gods before thyself.

Thou shalt not kill, or at least if thou art going to kill, thou shalt have a game of football with the thing thou is going to kill before thou properly finishest it off.

Thou shalt repeat the internal mantra 'I hate this! It's fucking great!' about the majority of life experiences.

Thou shalt not drink the water put out for thee by thy humans. Thou shalt instead demand to drink the freshest water in Christendom straight from the tap, although if that is not forthcoming, thou shalt protest by drinking any old rainy, algae-spattered crap thou might find in next door's garden.

Thou shalt ignore any toy thy human has bought for thee, especially the really expensive ones, but thou shalt dearly cherish the packaging of said toy, and have hours of fun with it.

Thou shalt forget thy mother and father quite quickly when separated from them, and, if thou happens to see them again, thou shalt sniff their bottoms then hiss at them intimidatingly.

Thou shalt snack voraciously, stealing at least one fish before the age of three, always remembering to leave something black and hard to remove behind after every meal, and getting irrationally excited when thy biscuit dispenser is topped up, even though thy new biscuits are just the same as those underneath.

Thou shalt not commit adultery, except in a kind of 'dry hump' way, with thy owner's cleanest knitwear and bedding.

Thou shalt not covet thy neighbour's cardboard box.

Thou shalt never forget the rule that thy affection towards thy human should rise and fall in direct proportion to the amount of miscellaneous crap stuck to thy fur at the time.

Sole Man

'In retrospect, perhaps I didn't quite think it through,' said Jamie.

He, Russ, Amy and I were sitting in our favourite pub in Norwich. On the table in front of us was a mousetrap. Jamie and Russ, who'd been best friends for more than two decades, were born only a day apart, and over the years they had developed a tradition of buying useful, unromantic birthday presents for one another – of which this was the latest.

'No, no. It's great,' protested Russ. 'I just wonder if there's a way of catching her *without* severing her spine.'

Three weeks ago, Russ's hamster, Baboushka, had escaped beneath the floorboards of his house. Now, with only a fortnight to go before he was due to move to the other side of the city, he was losing hope of finding her. In theory, Jamie's gift, which described itself as a 'humane, alternative' trap, was typically thoughtful and practical. It was only when you looked more closely – examined, for example, the drawing on the base of its packaging, depicting a mouse being hanged from a steel noose – that you began to wonder how well it would really work out in the long term for Baboushka.

'What about Tom's cats?' asked Jamie. 'Couldn't you borrow one of them? I hear they're very gentle.'

I hadn't told Russ and Jamie about my cats' recent fall from grace as mousers, but I wasn't surprised that word had reached them. Norwich is a small city, where gossip travels fast, and the transformation of Shipley and Ralph from habitual vole chompers to a kind of reliable family-run rodent bus service had been fairly spectacular. It was now three months since Janet's demise: precisely the period since I'd last seen a mouse's spleen on my carpets, let alone trodden in one. In a way, it was rather touching: their own special fourteen-week silence in memory of a cat who had never been truly interested in killing anything, with the exception of empty Frazzles packets.

It wasn't that Shipley and Ralph had stopped catching mice; they just seemed to have lost all their urgency in savaging them, instead leaving them unharmed behind sofas and cupboards, with what appeared to be a 'just in case' mentality. No longer did the patio resemble their own special mouseoleum. Always careful to keep a complete one around for later, their approach to rodents had become a little bit like a *Blue Peter* presenter's to cardboard dioramas.

I wouldn't have been entirely confident about lending

Ralph or Shipley to Russ. Even with their new approach to prey, there was still the odd mishap: a broken leg here, a miniature heart attack there. Mostly, however, I would manage to catch and free the victims early enough, using an oversized coffee mug I'd got free from the hi-fi shop Richer Sounds and an *All the President's Men* DVD case, while a reclining Shipley or Ralph raised a wry eyebrow in the background. I had no great sentimental attachment to the Richer Sounds mug, but I hadn't intended to use the case of *All the President's Men*, which was one of my favourite films of all time. It had, however, been the first item available on an occasion about six months ago when I'd successfully rescued a mouse Shipley had left by my DVD shelves, and I thought it best not to monkey with the formula. I performed these capture routines so often now, I'd begun to look at them in the way one might look upon an unpaid evening job for a local charity.

At least I had a warning system when there was a rodent on the way, in the form of Ralph's special Mouse Meow. This was different to his normal meow, which entailed a shout of 'RAAALLO!' or 'RAAAALPH!' It was more urgent and, if such a thing could be deemed feasible, even more self-satisfied. It was impressive that he could meow at all with a fresh mousetache across his face, but I think if he'd been really clever he would have invented another meow to differentiate between the times when he had brought a mouse in, the times when he had brought a vole in, and the times when he had brought a moorhen in.

I'd always purchased collars with large bells for Shipley and Ralph, to prevent them catching birds. Moorhens, fortunately, weren't a regular occurrence, but Ralph had somehow managed to drag one through the catflap a week ago, leaving it intact in my study to sit stunned for a moment then excrete its way dizzily around the carpet. I wasn't happy about it, but there's one good thing to be said about clearing up a room entirely spattered with viscous moorhen poo: it gives you a fairly revelatory appreciation of all the times in the past when you weren't.

Adjudicating 'disputes' between my cats and the creatures in my garden was all part of the peculiar madness that grips Norfolk every spring. It's the same madness that prompts an old man in the town where I live to stand at the edge of the lake and yell 'Come on then! Let's be 'avin' you!' at the ducks as he feeds them, the same madness that had caused a fisherman on the banks of the River Wensum in Norwich to bound up to me the previous week waving a camera and a bream and ask, 'Will you take a picture of me and my fish?' The moorhens that came into the garden were a sizeable element of the story, as were ducklings, and a muntjac deer Ralph had over-ambitiously tried to get a bit handy with when it was having an afternoon nap behind my pampas grass. I loved the county more than ever at this time of year. It was holidaying in Norfolk in the spring that had initially convinced me I could live here, and, if Janet's death had prompted any thoughts of starting again elsewhere, they were soon quashed by seeing the oil-seed rape appearing in the fields beside the back lanes, my garden coming into unkempt bloom, and taking a picnic in the sun under the shadow of Norwich Cathedral.

In the first few days after Janet's death I'd found it hard to shake an odd feeling: a strange conviction that I'd forgotten something, without being sure what, accompanied by a sense that, if I strained my mind hard enough, I could remember and somehow bring Janet back. It was a different feeling to the one I'd had directly after the previous cat death I'd experienced first hand: that of Brewer,

Ralph and Shipley's brother, in 2002. Back then, I'd been angry as well as devastated: half at myself for buying a first house next to precisely the wrong kind of road for a cat owner – one along which people drove very fast but was also subject to long periods of quiet that brought about a false sense of security – and half at the prison officer who'd run him over then raced off into the night, leaving my kind neighbour to rush Brewer hopelessly to the vet. Anger was not what I felt now, and my state of bereavement – though at first an enormously powerful sensation that had manifested itself deep in my chest – soon became more philosophical, with the fully dawning realisation that, of all the ways to go, Janet's surely had been one of the better ones, and, if he'd continued deteriorating for another year or two, he would probably not have been a happy cat.

His death, however, had left a hole in the house. It was like the hole the death of a widely loved, long-serving doorman might have left at a shabby hotel: the kind of person about whom an acquaintance might have remarked, 'I can't believe Jimmy's gone. I mean, I guess I never got to know the real him, but in a lot of ways you could say he *was* The Moorhen Astoria.'

I think I'd accepted Janet was no longer here. Or had I? When there were three cats in front of me eating I'd often catch myself whistling absent-mindedly for one more. For the time being, his pills remained in the kitchen drawer, the bottle three-quarters full. I wanted to find the owner of another cat who suffered from hyperthyroidism so I could pass them on, but it was a difficult topic to raise. How exactly would I put it? 'Hey! I've got some Jaffa Cakes in the cupboard. Would you like one? Also, do you fancy taking my dead cat's medication off my hands?'

Walking helped, enormously. In the weeks following Janet's death I hurled myself into the Norfolk countryside even more zealously than before, tramping along towpaths, past sluice gates and ruined monasteries, over stiles and through meadows in my threadbare walking boots, enjoying the feeling of surrendering myself to the elements, free of physical baggage. Sometimes I was joined for these walks by friends, or by Henry, a cocker spaniel owned by my friend Hannah who lived up the road: a somewhat Janet-like dog in both his uncomplicated approach to the world and his penchant for stagnant water. I was equally happy being alone, though. I loved the simplicity and purposeless of walking: you weren't trying to win a game, or prove anything, or to get ahead in life; you were just out in the air, putting one foot in front of the other for the sake of it. I'm sure it's possible to feel worse after a walk, but it had not happened to me in recent memory. I think, even though at one point I didn't realise it, I've always felt the same, right back to my late teens, when I went on three- or four-mile rambles in the Forestry Commission land behind my parents' old cottage in north Nottinghamshire with my childhood cat Monty. I told myself this was merely a way of killing time while I wasn't engaged in the much more crucial activity of interviewing rock bands, but it was actually one of the highlights of my week.

'MONTY WAS A BRILLIANT CAT,' my dad would often say in his extremely loud voice. 'THERE'LL PROBABLY NEVER BE ANOTHER ONE LIKE HIM.' My dad's tone seemed to imply that if you were a cat, you faced a choice early on in life: you either knuckled down, got a job and bettered yourself, or you lazed around and became one of society's drop-outs.

Monty, who died in 1998, was not my parents' last cat. Daisy, a tightly wound ball of tortoiseshell neuroses who'd served as Monty's whipping girl, had survived for nine further anxious years after his death, running from the sound of my dad's thunderous footsteps, occasionally offering my mum morsels of affection but arguably finding true companionship only with an old feather duster that my parents had bought in the Mansfield branch of Wilkinsons in 1990 (our theory was that she thought it was an uncommonly accommodating parrot). It was, though, Monty's gold standard of feline behaviour that mostly explained the catless state my mum and dad had lived in for the last three and a half years. He was the kind of supremely confident, outdoorsy, no-nonsense cat you might find in a Victorian children's story, and I could understand why you wouldn't want to try to replace him. In more recent years, though, there'd always seemed to be something missing when I visited my parents' house, and I saw it as my job to campaign for change. It had been six years since I'd last had a kitten in my life. With Janet's passing still so recent, I wasn't quite ready for another of my own, but that wasn't to say I wasn't ready for another of *their* own.

'I think it's time,' I would say to my mum.

'Neh,' she would reply. 'I'm really enjoying how clean the house is at the moment.'

'I feel you could really benefit from it.'

'Maybe. But, if I get one, how will I know it's a good one?'

'Most of them are good ones, as long as you treat them well.'

'Hmm. Maybe. But, no, I'm fine.'

I could see the cracks beginning to show, though, especially on the occasions when she visited my house. 'You've got too many cats. You need two, at the most. I'll have this one,' she'd say, picking The Bear up. The Bear, having long since deemed my mum of sufficient intellect to be worthy of his affection, could not resist a stand-up cuddle. He would begin to purr, and cling to her with his koala-like claws. 'He's a good one. And Shipley's always bullying him.'

It was true: Shipley did give The Bear a hard time, but I could never quite convince myself it was a hard enough one to justify a permanent separation. Shipley would sometimes donk The Bear on the head, but mostly his specific brand of cowardly aggression involved turfing The Bear off a warm spot he quite fancied himself, or dancing about in front of him, pulling the obnoxious faces of a feline punk. Being a cat who believed strongly in non-violence, The Bear never once retaliated, instead relying on his sole defence: the ability to make the noise of a small dragon gargling with lighter fluid.

'Eweeeeegggghhh!' Shipley would say to The Bear,

dancing about in front of his face in the kind of way that, were he human and in a nightclub, would probably soon result in someone punching him in the neck.

'Aaaargle baaargle aaargle,' The Bear would reply, and scuttle behind the sofa.

It wasn't pretty to watch, but normally their exchange of opinions escalated no further.

That was, however, immaterial. *This was The Bear we were talking about, for goodness' sake.* He was the best cat in the universe. Of course, there were times when I thought *all* of my cats were the best cat in the universe, but, from a purely objective point of view, The Bear really *was* the best. Yes, he might have peed on my curtains a couple of times recently, and there had been, in the dark early years, the incident with the turd and Dee's dressing gown pocket, but on the whole, no cat had a sweeter nature. As if to underline this, he even had a white patch on his chest in the shape of a wonky heart, like a per-manent badge of his sensitivity. He was a complex, superior being, and it took time to understand him. My mum might have thought she was ready for that, but she would probably feel different when she'd spent a couple of days being followed around by him, with those deep, watery pupils making a thousand pressing queries of her. It took nerves of steel to cope with that kind of thing. Even after more than a decade of knowing him, it would often be all I could do not to pop down the local park with a crate full of extra-strength lager after seeing him materialise out of nowhere next to my chair, his question-mark eyes boring deep into me. Besides, for my parents to adopt The Bear would be breaking the unspoken law that surrounded him. The next person to own The Bear would have to be my next ex-partner. These were the rules, and they were now very firmly established.

Actually, I could see one good reason why my mum and dad were reluctant to get a new cat, and might only want a special, pacifist one, such as The Bear: their garden had become more of a wildlife haven than ever in recent years. I may have had moorhens and muntjac in mine, but I had not quite managed to cultivate a close personal relationship with either, as my mum and dad seemed to have done with the fish, frogs, toads, black-birds and woodpeckers living at their place. Barely a day seemed to go by without a text update from my mum of another intense brush with wildlife. Sometimes, the action was not even limited to the outside of the house.

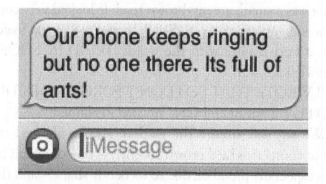

Not long after I'd most recently arrived at their front door, my dad had taken me to one side. 'TOM, CAN I HAVE A WORD?' he'd said.

When my dad says 'TOM, CAN I HAVE A WORD?' it usually means one of three things: a) he's about to ask me if I've completed my tax return, b) he wants to know if I've got my car ready for winter yet, or c) he wants to warn me to 'WATCH OUT FOR FOOKWITS AND NUTTERS' next time I go out. This time, though, his agenda was different. He led me into the porch and pointed at a rack that contained various gardening footwear – some of which, from what I could gather, dated from as far back as 1946.

'I'VE GOT A TOAD LIVING IN MY SHOE,' he said.

I bent down to look at his slip-on gardening loafers: the same gripless shoes he'd worn, in defiance of my mum's wishes, to climb and prune a tree in the pouring rain fifteen months ago, as a consequence of which he had fallen to the ground, several feet below, and broken his spine. Sure enough, tucked up cosily inside the left shoe was a small, greeny-brown toad. It looked very content – complacent, even. Stuck to the toe of the loafer was a Post-it note with the words 'TOAD IN SHOE!' scrawled upon it.

'I WROTE THAT SO I DON'T FORGET AND TRY TO PUT THE SHOE ON,' my dad explained.

We strolled around the garden, and he showed me some courgettes he'd grown recently – one of which he was especially proud of, due to its bendy shape – and the netting he'd put over the pond to keep a meddling neighbourhood heron from stealing his koi carp. 'IT'S AN ABSOLUTE BASTARD,' he told me. 'IT'S STILL HANGING AROUND EVEN NOW.' Last week, he

explained, the heron had caught his favourite fish, Finn, then dropped his lifeless body from the air. I sensed from the chalk outline he'd drawn in the exact shape of Finn's body on the flagstones next to the pond that he was taking the loss hard, and I found it difficult to come up with the right words of comfort.

'He's in a better place now.'

'WHAT? IN THE GROUND UNDER YOUR MUM'S CORDYLINE PLANT?'

'No, I mean fish heaven, or wherever it is they go.'

We moved towards the shed. 'THERE WAS ANOTHER TOAD, TOO,' he said. 'THAT ONE USED TO LIVE OVER HERE IN THE COMPOST HEAP. I USED TO PUT A BLANKET OVER IT AND TUCK IT IN AT NIGHT. HAVE YOU FIXED YOUR CONSERVATORY ROOF YET? DON'T GO UP THERE YOURSELF. KEITH HARRIS AND HIS DUCK ORVILLE DIED DOING THAT.'

Later that evening, my mum fed me a stupendously tasty meal, combined, apparently, with at least three other stupendously tasty meals to compensate for all the times I hadn't visited her recently. Meanwhile my dad talked about the writer Martin Amis, who was the same age as him, and the different opportunities the two of them had in their lives, due to their contrasting roots.

'WHEN MARTIN AMIS WAS EIGHT, HE SAW HIS DAD SHARING PROFOUND THOUGHTS WITH PHILIP LARKIN,' my dad said. 'WHEN I WAS EIGHT, I SAW MY UNCLE KEN SHARING SOME CHEESE WITH HIS ALSATIAN, BRUCE.'

Somehow, in the way that these things can when my dad is speaking, this led into an anecdote about the walk he'd been on with my mum in Leicestershire last week. 'WE STOPPED FOR A NAP IN A FIELD BUT I WOKE UP BECAUSE A COW WAS LICKING ME,' he said. 'I THOUGHT IT WAS YOUR MUM KISS-ING ME BUT IT WAS A COW LICKING ME.' As we cleared away the dirty plates, the door knocker sounded. I'd expected it to be Roger and Bea, the extremely lovely, extremely elderly couple next door who would often drive the forty yards from their back door to the end of their garden to eat their tea in their greenhouse, and some-times take a detour to see my mum and dad on the way. I was surprised, however, to see the white ghost of a kitten, sitting in the porch at head height, and peering in at us.

'Casper!' said my mum, opening the door, picking up the ghost and peppering his head with kisses. 'How are you? You're beautiful, aren't you? Yesyouare.'

The kitten seemed to enjoy the kisses, which sug-gested he was a corporeal, living form after all, and could actually feel this stuff. As he received them, he beamed in a way that seemed to say 'Because I'm worth it'.

I looked at the two of them quizzically.

'Oh, erm, yes,' said my mum. 'This is Casper. He lives next door. He's learned to climb up and tap the door knocker with his paw.'

I gave Casper a scratch on the head. He looked up and assessed me lazily. It was a very different look to those soul-piercing ones The Bear gave me. This look was full of sleepy entitlement, as if, to Casper, my face was just another blurry, unspecific, adoring mass of skin. He seemed like a big softy: a cat full of trust, who was very assured of his place in the world. There was something familiar about him. I couldn't quite place it at first, but then it hit me: if you added a few sandy patches, what you would have was an almost exact replica of a four- or five-month-old Monty. It was all there, from the confident aura to the sense that, if he was a person, his wardrobe would probably have favoured britches.

My mum poured a tiny bit of crème fraîche into a bowl for him, and he lapped it up enthusiastically. 'I know I'm not supposed to,' she said. 'I just give it him very occasionally. Oh look, he's left a heart in it just for me.'

She was right: where Casper had lapped at the crème fraîche, it had separated to make almost exactly the shape of a picture-book love heart. It was impressive, but, living with a cat who had a fur heart on his chest, I was perhaps a little less overawed than many others might have been.

Over the next few weeks, various photographs from my mum arrived via email, chronicling Casper's adventures in their garden: Casper strutting across their lawn, as if slightly behind schedule on his way to give an important PowerPoint presentation; Casper in the foreground, casually cleaning himself, as my dad chopped logs, shirtless, in the background; Casper in a tree, looking down on my mum and dad's vegetable patch as if certain he had planted and tended the potatoes in it himself. My mum sent me other photos, but sometimes even these had a subliminal Casper theme. When she emailed me a picture of a lovely, new, log-cabin quilt she'd been sewing, it took me a while to evaluate the needlework and colour scheme, as I'd been distracted by the white cat sprawled contentedly upon it.

After a month of this, I decided it was time to telephone her and have a serious chat.

'I'LL JUST GET HER,' my dad said. 'SHE'S OUTSIDE WITH MONTY. I FELL ASLEEP IN THE COMPOST AGAIN.'

'Hold on. What did you just say?'

'I SAID I FELL ASLEEP IN THE COMPOST AGAIN.'

'No, not that bit. The other bit.'

'SHE'S OUTSIDE WITH CASPER.'

'Yeah, but that's not what you said, is it? You said "She's outside with Monty".'

'DID I? OH, THAT'S WEIRD. HE'S A GOOD CAT, THAT ONE. YOU DON'T GET MANY LIKE HIM.'

'It works out well,' my mum told me a few minutes later. 'He pops along every so often and we have a cuddle, but I don't have to spend money on cat food, or spend my life cleaning up paw prints or other cat mess.'

I wondered if my mum was being honest with herself. When she'd visited my house the previous week I'd noticed a distinct glaze of white fuzz on the black jumper she was wearing.

'Are you sure it wouldn't just be best to get a cat of your own? There are lots of lovely homeless ones out there, just waiting to put a heart in your crème fraîche.'

'Oh, it would be nice. But I'd only want one if it was as nice as Monty. Sorry, I mean Casper. And how would I know he was? I could never be sure.'

I was worried about the potential repercussions if my parents got too attached to their neighbours' cat – it seemed likely to end in tears, one way or another – but I had a plan. It was a long shot, whose many elements might take a little time to put properly in place, but I was working on it.

From the time of Janet's death, I'd been noticing some very strange goings-on upstairs in the Upside Down House. In the morning, arriving in the kitchen, I would find that many of the cat biscuits I'd left out had vanished – far more than my cats would normally eat. If you were an imaginative sort of person, you might even say that it was as if they had been magically moved from their place in the dispenser to a giant, invisible stomach. Reaching for a loaf I'd bought the previous day, I'd find its seal broken and one of the corners nibbled off. Later, moving across to my vinyl collection to pull out *Still Bill*, the 1972 album by Bill Withers – which, despite purchasing a whole twelve years earlier, I never felt I'd given the love it deserved – I would find it freshly covered in sticky, yellow liquid. Another morning, I found a similar liquid on the blackboard where I wrote my weekly shopping lists: a critical wet streak going diagonally through the words 'fabric conditioner'.

Even if I had been a devout believer in the spirit world, I could not have suspected that any of these were the acts of Ghost Janet. He had never been the most creative pisser, and, if he had to come back and soil any of my records, I think it would far more likely have been something which had regularly troubled his eardrums in his lifetime – Deep Purple's *Fireball*, perhaps, or the first Uriah Heep LP. My doubts were confirmed a week later when, coming upstairs to get a drink of water, I found a ginger cat sneakily munching from one of the biscuit dispensers. You might argue that 'sneakily' is the wrong word to use about any activity that involves making the noise 'ORRGOBNRRROMGOBNROMMGOBBLE-GORBLE', but he'd certainly been stealthy upon entering the house and he made his getaway in a blur of streetwise determination.

Since then, I'd been keeping an eye out for the ginger intruder, but he was always very careful, timing his raids to coincide with the occasions when I was asleep or watching television downstairs. If I caught him in the act, he'd shoot past me, hurdling banisters and other cats, not letting me get a proper look at his face. I began taking photos of him when I saw him from a distance, poking his head around the corner of the house's lower staircase, or stopping to stare back at me, seemingly with regret, as he scuttled off down the garden steps, but these cameraphone snaps always came out blurry. I began to wonder if it had nothing to do with the photographs at all and he was just a very blurry cat.

My plan was going to take a bit longer than I'd anticipated. If I was to befriend this cat, rehabilitate him and turn up on my mum's doorstep and present him to her as an irresistible reintroduction to cat ownership, to take her focus away from Casper, it was going to be a matter of baby steps: a sort of 'softly, softly, catchy thieving furry urchin' approach. Finding out what his face looked like would be a start. I had observed enough of his behaviour to know that, if my plan came to fruition, I wouldn't be stealing someone else's cat, though – or that I would at most be stealing someone else's very neglected cat. He must have been hungry, since every night he began to meow outside the door pathetically. He had one of those throaty Rod Stewart meows that ginger cats often have, except in this case it was more like the kind of noise Rod Stewart would make if he was being forced to sing while suffering from the recent swine flu bug.

'Andrew!' I'd call, gently opening the door and offering him some biscuits. From a distance, he seemed like an Andrew to me: he had that same aura that a lot of Andrews have of knowing a lot of people and being very punctual.

'Eweeeeaaagggggh,' Andrew would say again, from somewhere in the darkness, and vanish.

Andrew clearly wanted to do this on his terms: he desired my food, but didn't want the damage incurred to his pride if he admitted that he was taking a handout. However, we both knew the score. If I was absolutely determined for him not to eat my cats' food, I could have done something about it. Andrew needed to be frank with himself: this was charity, whichever way he looked at it.

I'd had quite a few such visits from feline intruders in the past, and I wondered if word tended to get out about me in the feral community. I could picture the scene: two mangy tomcats sitting by some bins. 'I'm telling you, dude,' says one. 'This guy is a *pushover*. I heard he gave an old velvet jacket and a lamp to the PDSA last week that he could have got at least twenty quid each for on eBay. No magnetic lock on the catflap. His ex didn't suffer fools gladly, but she's not there any more, and he suffers fools *extremely* gladly. Lives all on his own. Leaves biscuits out all night in huge dispensers. Often has some rubbish Deep Purple album on really loud, so he probably won't even hear you come in. You can gorge yourself to your heart's content.'

'But doesn't he live with that big fluffy black guy? The one with the girl's name? Jean, or something.'

'Janet, you mean? Nope. You're all clear now. He popped his clogs weeks ago. The only ones left are so spoilt they won't care if you go in there. They don't even kill mice any more. Just bring them in as if they want them to be their friends or something. The little one with the white heart as a bib has never killed anything in his whole life, apart from this spider he sat on once, and he felt bad about that for months.'

I could not avoid noticing that Ralph, Shipley and The Bear had displayed a notable indifference to Andrew. Shipley had made a petulant teenage 'eeeaAAEEGH' noise a couple of times as Andrew scuttled past him towards the catflap, but Shipley made a petulant teenage 'eeeaAAEEGH' noise at me at least once every hour. He'd even made it at a jar of budget crunchy peanut butter I bought from Asda the previous week. It didn't necessarily signify anything. Once, on his way out, Andrew hurdled straight over the back of The Bear who – far too intellectual to reduce himself to violence, as always – just looked up at me as if to say, 'Now this. *Really?*' The apathy of Ralph, the biggest and ostensibly the toughest of my cats, was perhaps most surprising of all. Pablo had been a ginger and, not long before he left to live with Dee, there had been times when his and Ralph's enmity had escalated into something verging on race war. But now Ralph barely opened an eye as Andrew came in and did his stuff.

One night I woke at around 3 a.m. to the sound of aggrieved meowing, and raced into the living room, thinking that my cats had finally decided that they were mad as hell and weren't going to take it any more. What I found were two moggies fighting behind the curtains, neither of whom were mine. Even more surprisingly, neither of them was Andrew. I still didn't know precisely what his face looked like but I knew it was neither a) white, with a moustache, nor b) a kind of weird tortoiseshell/tabby mix, with crazy eyes on top.

Many years ago, when I first moved to Norfolk, I'd found a couple of other strange feral cats fighting behind my curtains. I hadn't really enjoyed it at the time, but as the months passed I'd come to remember it somewhat fondly. Back in the heat of the moment again, though, I spluttered in an exasperated manner, asking the pair of them ineffectually what on earth they thought they were doing. 'This isn't a cat YMCA I run here, you know,' I added, ineffectually. They each gave me a snarl and slunk off, still bashing one another around the head on the way out: less, seemingly, because they had any anger left towards one another and more as one last gesture of defiance towards me.

I began to revise my plan. Perhaps I wouldn't give Andrew to my mum after all, but would keep him for my very own, training him to defend the house from other intruder cats, in lieu of the services of Ralph, Shipley and The Bear? I wondered just how much work the ailing Janet had been doing on the battle lines, without me realising it. I'd perhaps been fooled by his easy-going nature around my other cats into thinking he was like that with all his peers. My remaining three moggies' approach to socialising could not be more different to his: they were kind of antisocial with one another, but took a live-and-let-live approach with the other cats in the neighbourhood.

While their territorial pride remained somewhat piti-ful, by summer Ralph and Shipley had, to say the least, started to make up for their post-Janet no-kill vigil of spring. Arriving on the patio to breathe the fresh morning air, I would enjoy only a few seconds of tran-quillity before it was punctured by the sight of that night's vole cull. The quarter of my garden nearest the house once again took on the feel of a mouseoleum and I gave thanks that I'd not been talked into a loan arrangement to help Russ with Baboushka (sadly, he'd moved house without ever finding her). In June, a wood pigeon crashed fatally into the living-room window, and I couldn't help wondering if it was suicide, prompted by the carnage below. The same month, whilst gardening, I found a dead squirrel in one of the beds near the window of my study, a rictus of fright on its face. This was a surprisingly big scalp for my cats by the sedate hunting standards of their middle years, so perhaps it could be put down to Andrew. Either that, or it had died from sheer shock at realising what a massive prat Shipley was.

'IT'S LIKE A FOOKIN' ABATTOIR OUT HERE,' said my dad. He and my mum had come to stay for a couple of days and help me do some gardening. 'GOD, WHO WOULD HAVE CATS? YOU SHOULD LET YOUR MUM TAKE ONE OF THEM. GIVE HER THAT ONE WHO'S ALWAYS LOOKING AT ME.'

I had never quite been able to work out what The Bear thought of my dad. Whenever he saw him, he looked

more quizzical than ever. He was a very discerning
animal, very particular about the kind of humans he con-
sorted with, and, over the years, I'd got a good measure of
the type of person he preferred. If you were a privileged or
vacuous sort, he wasn't really interested in you. If, however, you had a tendency to worry and some kind of
struggle in your past, he would be at your side in no time,
staring up at you with his heartbroken owl eyes.

My dad, who'd grown up poor on a council estate and
had told me just yesterday, as I climbed into the loft, 'BE
CAREFUL – OVER TWO THOUSAND PEOPLE IN
BRITAIN DIE FALLING OUT OF LOFTS EVERY
YEAR,' definitely fit the latter profile. But there was the
slight problem of volume. The Bear's sixteen-year-old eye-
sight was a little suspect, but his hearing was a thing of
genuine, undimmed wonder. If I had a turkey treat for him
and wanted to give him the chance to eat it alone,
unswamped by other, more greedy felines, all I had to do
was say his name in a tiny whisper from several feet away,
and he'd be there, by the fridge. When you have ears like
that, it must be difficult to be around my dad, a man whose
sneeze alone is so loud that, as a teenager, I'd occasionally
be able to hear it when playing football in the garden of my
friend Matthew Spittal, who lived seventeen doors away.

'IS THAT WHERE YOUR OTHER CAT IS
BURIED?' my dad asked, pointing to a seven-foot by
four-foot area of loamy soil I'd recently dug out, not far
from the apple tree.

'No, that's going to be a vegetable patch.'

'OH RIGHT. I WAS GOING TO SAY, I KNEW HE

WAS A BIG CAT BUT I DIDN'T THINK HE WAS THAT BIG.'

I took the dead squirrel to the lake at the end of the garden, and gave it a watery burial. The Bear watched searchingly from under the willow tree nearby. Was he judging me? It seemed somehow wrong to throw a squirrel in a lake, but also infinitely preferable to the first alternative that sprang to mind: putting it in the bin. Mary would have approved of my actions: everything going back to the earth, whether it be dead squirrel or cat sick. Or, as was the case here, going back to the litter-strewn lake bed. As I dropped it into the water, I saw a big fish with a moustache swim over past an empty Lilt can to check it out.

'IS IT OK IF I GARDEN IN MY PANTS?' I could hear my dad asking my mum. Standing several yards away, on The Bear's balcony, he was topless, with his T-shirt wrapped around his head in the form of a bandanna, which probably explained why The Bear wasn't up there. I couldn't hear my mum's response, but I sensed – and hoped – it was in the negative.

'BUT WHY NOT? IT'S OK. NOBODY CAN SEE ME.' My dad's point was rendered somewhat moot by the fact that, while they wouldn't be able to see him, my neighbours – probably about forty-six of them, in total – would almost certainly by now have heard him.

As an adult, I'd always been stubborn about accepting help from my parents. I'd only ever borrowed money from them once, and even then had paid them back later the same afternoon – and I was determined for it to stay that way. Now, however, my house and the space sur-rounding it was overwhelming me more than ever. Additionally, I'd lost a couple of my main forms of income, as free online content forced newspapers to cut pages. In the last year, in my more downbeat moments, I had often felt like all the smooth-running constituent parts of my house I'd taken selfishly for granted for years had got together and agreed to fall to bits at the same time, at exactly the point when I was suffering the finan-cial consequences of a mortgage buyout and loss of work. There were surprises everywhere. Who knew, for exam-ple, that if you didn't check the ivy on the side of your house properly for a year or two, it could climb through your walls and attack your boiler, costing you almost a thousand pounds to put right? Two months ago, I'd woken in the night to the sound of rain gushing into my conservatory through a crack in the roof. With the aid of a mop, some gaffer tape and almost every towel in the house, I'd cleaned up and minimised the damage, but I knew it would only take another deluge for it to happen again, possibly with even more catastrophic results.

This latter mishap could not be put down to wear and tear alone. When Andrew arrived in the evening, he always did so via the conservatory roof, which was made of cheap Perspex. His repeated landings in the same spot, which were heavy as a brick and often caused me to shoot bolt upright from a deep sleep, had clearly taken their toll. I opted not to tell my parents this, though, as I didn't want to tarnish their view of Andrew before they had met him. In over-ambitious flights of fancy, I'd envisaged that this weekend's visit might be the one when I presented him to them, but at present they were still unaware of his existence, and it seemed better, for the time being, that it should stay that way. I still had lots of work to do on his behaviour – trying to get him to come near me, for example, or not to meow like he had an extreme case of laryngitis.

Outside, there was even more to take care of. My shed now had no door, and leaned so severely that it was half in Deborah and David's garden. The small, ancient wooden jetty leading out over the polluted water of the lake had decayed to the extent that, standing gingerly on it to give the squirrel its send-off, I'd run a serious risk of finding out what someone living in medieval Fenland might have thought of as a weekend spa break. Earlier in the year, a dead tree that my mum had warned me about – warnings I'd summarily ignored – had crashed down in high winds over the path leading to the lawn. With the wet spring, and the lack of care I'd given it over the preceding three years, the rest of the garden ominously previewed a future age where men have surrendered completely to the will of plants.

'MY MATE DAVE BLACKWELL SAYS IF YOU HAVE ONE OF THESE IT MEANS YOU'RE INTO WIFE SWAPPING,' said my dad, as we chopped back my out-of-control pampas grass.

The noisy gardener/quiet gardener dynamic had worked for many years for my mum and dad now, but I did wonder if, somewhere in the back of my mum's mind, there was a fantasy parallel existence where she and BBC

Gardeners' World presenter Monty Don sat beneath a weeping willow, sharing lemon drizzle cake and gently discussing deadheading. I think perhaps my dad was aware of this too, as was evinced on the one occasion they'd met Monty Don. Last year in the car park, after a spoken-word event hosted by Don, my mum had come a little too close to reversing their car into the famous gardener. 'SORRY ABOUT THAT,' my dad had told him. 'SHE BLOOMIN' LOVES YOU. SHE WOULD HAVE BEEN HEARTBROKEN IF SHE'D KILLED YOU.'

My mum is so green-fingered, her hands are virtually a form of foliage in themselves. If there's nobody around to stop her, she'll garden until it's too dark to see the fronds right in front of her face. My dad, meanwhile, has never been one to do things by half, or even by three-quarters, and, at sixty-two, would throw himself into any physical activity as if the digits in his age were the wrong way around. But neither of my parents were in the best of health, and I worried about them. 'I'LL BE FINE,' said my dad, when I voiced my concern about him climbing six feet to saw off part of the dead tree that was still standing. 'I'LL BE FINE' was, I couldn't help but recall, exactly what he'd said to my mum eighteen months previously, just before he'd fallen out of that tree in their garden and come within a couple of millimetres of ending up paralysed for the rest of his life. That said, doom unto others as you doom unto yourself was not part of his philosophy. 'WHATEVER YOU DO, DON'T PUT THAT SAW DOWN AND TAKE YOUR SHOES OFF THEN STAND ON IT,' he said to me as I began to cut a branch, even though I had expressed no wish or plan to take my shoes off. 'BE CAREFUL WITH THAT LIGHTER FLUID,' he said as I started the bonfire; two minutes later, he was throwing an amount onto it roughly equal to the amount of water you might throw on a bonfire of the same size if you wanted to put it out.

As my mum weeded and my dad and I sawed and burned the dead tree, Shipley sprinted around the garden ecstatically, shooting up and down Janet's apple tree and clapping the back of my bare legs with his paws in protest when I went back into the house to fetch drinks for everyone. He and Ralph had always loved it when I was in the garden; even if they were in a deep sleep in the most distant part of the house, they had a telepathic way of knowing when I'd gone outside, and would join me within a matter of seconds. If I was honest with myself, this was one of my main reasons for putting my financial concerns to one side and staying in The Upside Down House: the cats loved it. Previously I'd lived in houses that didn't suit my cats, but the Upside Down House ticked all the boxes. Indoors, they had plenty of space to ignore each other. Out of doors, they had a spacious hillside – or hillockside, this being Norfolk – to play on, with its own supply of takeaway food, yet it was also an enclosed environment that discouraged wanderlust. As a younger cat, The Bear had liked to roam, but now he was too arthritic to shin up over the front fence to the road, and Shipley and Ralph had long since cottoned on to the fact that all the good places to be were at the back of the house, not the front, where the cars were.

Maybe I could find another house like this, but it would not be easy. It was obvious to me that the main reason for the recent improvement in The Bear's health and happiness was that he had gone seven years without moving house. He'd been forced to move umpteen times in his sixteen or so lives and had always loathed it, often staging magical disappearances just as contracts were exchanged or tenancy agreements were signed. I didn't want to put him through that again. He'd shown early on in our friendship that he was a fiercely independent cat, perfectly capable of upping sticks if a situation wasn't to his liking, but after his early vanishing acts, somewhere along the way he seemed to have put his complete trust in me to dictate his future. Because of that, it seemed the least I could do to make him my priority. But could I cope, in a house I couldn't afford, needing more maintenance than I could manage?

One of the good things about hard physical work is that it makes you so tired you stop worrying about all these things, and that night, not long after my mum and dad and I stumbled in from the garden, I fell into a deep sleep. Andrew might have thumped down onto the conservatory roof in the early hours, but if he did, I was too comatose to be aware of it.

'I'VE FED THE CATS,' my dad told me the next morning, as I arrived in the kitchen. On the counter were three empty food sachets: three times as much as I normally gave The Bear, Shipley and Ralph in the morning as an addition to the biscuits in their dispenser. On the floor were a variety of dishes, only three of which were actually intended for cats. 'THE BIGGER ONE OUT OF THE TWO BLACK ONES TRIED TO EAT THE OTHERS' FOOD.'

'Thanks. Yes, that happens quite a lot.'

'NOT THIS ONE.' He pointed to The Bear, who was sitting on his favourite step stool, looking a little bemused. 'HE'S A GOOD ONE. IS THAT THE ONE YOUR MUM WANTS? YOU SHOULD GIVE HIM TO US. I THINK I'VE LEFT MY CHOCOLATE UNDER THE CUSHION ON YOUR SETTEE. I HIDE IT FROM MYSELF UNDER SETTEE CUSHIONS SO IT'S FUN TO FIND LATER. SORRY IF I'VE MADE THE SETTEE STICKY.'

I inspected the coffee pot on the kitchen counter: in the bottom of it was a thick slick of coffee, suggesting that my dad had ground approximately the amount of beans I do in, say, a fortnight. I knew the caffeine wouldn't make much difference to him. In the comic-book series, Asterix, Asterix's best friend Obelix has no need for the magic potion that Asterix's tribe drink; having fallen into a cauldron of it when he was a baby, he has since been permanently under its spell. My theory had long been that something similar had happened to my dad in his childhood with an unusually large urn of coffee, meaning that he now operated permanently on the level that most people attain only after six or seven cups of the stuff.

'I'VE BEEN UP SINCE FIVE,' he said. My dad tells me he's 'BEEN UP SINCE FIVE' a lot, but in this instance the information was superfluous. I already knew he'd been up since five, as I'd been up since five too, having been woken by the sound of him loudly clucking at next door's chickens.

'HAVE YOU SEEN THE GARDEN TROWEL ANY-WHERE?'

My dad often drinks whisky before bedtime, but this never seems to have any effect on him the next day, and he's at his most garrulous early in the morning. I'm a morning person, but I'm slower to get my head together. When he stays over, I can sometimes find it a bit much.

'CAN YOU PUT ROLLING NEWS ON THE TELLY FOR ME?' he continued. 'I ALWAYS WATCH ROLLING NEWS AT THIS TIME IN THE MORN-ING WHEN I'M AT HOME. EITHER THAT, OR I LISTEN TO SOME BLUES OR JAZZ REALLY LOUD. DID I EVER TELL YOU ABOUT WHAT MY MATE JEFF WOULD DO IN THE SIXTIES? AFTER A BATH HE'D PUT ON HIS ELECTRIC BLANKET AND LIE ON IT SMOKING AND LISTENING TO HOWLIN' WOLF SONGS UNTIL HE WAS DRY. WHEN YOUR MUM FIRST CAME TO MY HOUSE I BORROWED PHIL DAY'S COLLECTION OF JAZZ LPS AND PRETENDED THEY WERE MINE. SHE DIDN'T EVEN NOTICE. DOES THAT TOASTER WORK? I COULDN'T GET IT TO MAKE TOAST.'

This would all have been discombobulating enough, but seeing, in the middle of it, a small toad hopping across the kitchen floor in the direction of the cat biscuit dispenser, made it more so.

'FOOKIN' 'ELL,' said my dad. 'LOOK! IT MUST HAVE BEEN LONELY AND WANTED TO COME WITH US. I SAY, JO, COME UP HERE AND GER A LOOK AT THIS!'

As my mum – who's always been a great friend to amphibians – caught the toad in her hands, and I went to fetch my dad's gardening loafers from the box in the hallway, The Bear continued to watch from his stool. I might have been mistaken, but his eyes looked even more saucer-like than usual. 'I didn't realise it at the time, but we normally have a fairly quiet life, don't we?' they seemed to be saying to me.

He stayed in position, while the other three of us gathered around the toad. 'IF YOU PUT IT IN THE HALL IT COULD BE TOAD OF TOAD HALL,' said my dad.

Later, when we'd placed the gardening loafers, complete with toad, in a quiet corner behind the house, my mum would recall that she'd checked the shoes thoroughly before leaving the previous morning, and found them empty. 'It must have hopped back into them between then and when your dad packed the car,' she reasoned. My dad had decided to garden in his trainers the previous day. Had he not done so, he would have discovered it earlier – perhaps in a way that, for him *and* for the toad, would have been more dramatic. Even so, we would have had the same dilemma: What do you do with a toad who's 116 miles from home, even though the toad has become a friend of sorts, when you don't really know much about the toad, and its wants and desires, and what really makes it tick?

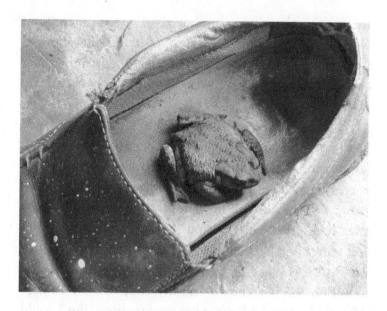

All I can say, looking back, is that we did what we thought best at the time. We had planned to spend that day out, and it seemed wrong to put the toad in the car or keep him locked up in the house. I knew, from my experiences at my very frog-friendly previous house, that Ralph, Shipley and The Bear had little interest in amphibians, and being back in the loafer gave the toad the choice: he could stay home, or he could explore his new environment. As it turned out, he decided to be brave. When we returned that evening, the loafer was empty, and it remained so the following morning, when my parents left. But I worried about him. Norfolk was culturally quite different to Nottinghamshire: life moved at a slower pace here and, especially towards the west of the county, there was a unique river system to contend with. What if he didn't settle in, or found himself missing my mum and dad's koi carp, Casper the friendly ghost cat, even the evil heron who liked to circle above the pond?

I'd expected the area surrounding my house to be at least one animal lighter by now, but the opposite had happened. Both Andrew and the toad were now out there somewhere. Who knew if their future would be here, with me, or with my parents, or elsewhere? Maybe they had already met. I hoped, if they had, that their encounter had been amicable. I certainly knew Andrew was still around. A couple of fresh streaks of urine I'd found on the blackboard and my copy of Neil Young's *After the Goldrush* LP served as confirmation. But I could deal with Andrew later. There was still plenty of work to do on that front.

'What was that?' my mum asked, the evening before they left, when he meowed throatily outside the living room.

'Oh,' I replied. 'It's just the wind. It sometimes makes that sound when it whistles through the hole in the conservatory roof.'

Five Highly Unlikely Pet Memoirs

Dickie: A Very Special Library Toad

One snowy morning, Beverley, a librarian due to retire in a few weeks and nursing a cynicism only exacerbated by recent government cuts to funding, goes to empty the drop box at the small town library where she works and finds a diminutive toad on top of a copy of *The Wind in the Willows*, which it appears to have been reading to keep its mind off the cold. 'Some *people*,' Beverley tuts, thinking that the toad has probably been abandoned by cruel owners who neglected to get their original family toad neutered. Despite having little previous experience with amphibians, she names the toad Dickie, and he soon becomes a well-known and well-loved character around the library, sitting on the shoulders of children as they read, splashing about in the sinks in the gents' toilets and building a toad nest for himself in the back of the photocopier, using old, scrunched-up, unwanted copies of church newsletters. Dickie's happy-go-lucky approach to life persuades Beverley to delay her retirement and reach an inner peace about her estrangement from her father, who ran off with the owner of a fish and chip van when she was seven.

Bartholomew and Me (and the Awkward Space Between Us)

One snowy night, Bartholomew, a cuddly marmalade cat with 'whiskers that won't quit', rolls up, as if out of nowhere, at the door of Kenneth, a lifelong bachelor who has never quite learned to love and has instead retreated to a tumbledown cottage on the North Devon coast and a solitary life of boatbuilding. Before Bartholomew arrives, for reasons largely down to a secret, repressed childhood trauma, Kenneth has begun to view wood with the affection that most people reserve for the living, and his few friends worry gravely about him. 'What's your name?' says Kenneth, upon Bartholomew's mysterious arrival. But Bartholomew doesn't answer, since he is a cat, and therefore can't speak English. Kenneth feeds Bartholomew some evaporated milk, and, with an almost human sigh, the feline beds down on the sofa for the night on an old blanket given to Kenneth by his beloved late grandma. The next day, Bartholomew leaves, and Kenneth's life resumes in precisely the same fashion as before.

Smug Puppies

Three rescue puppies arrive in Britain from Afghanistan and proceed to heal a broken family. Unfortunately, the broken family gets irritated with their do-gooding ways and gives them away to a friend of the completely intact family who live next door but one.

John: A Pretty Sodding Ordinary Owl
John, a snowy owl, moves in with Martha, a bereaved schoolteacher. Together, they set off on a road trip around America, visiting historical spots and meeting other birdlife. John, however, turns out to have very little personality, and mostly just stares off into space, or refuses to get out of Martha's Honda Civic. Things reach crisis point when, faced with the world's biggest giant redwood, all he can do is emit a pellet whilst looking shirty.

David, the Massive Satanic Goat
Jim, a writer who has has experienced success on the bestseller list with his books *Walking My Dog in North Yorkshire*, *Walking My Dog in South Yorkshire* and *Walking My Dog in West Yorkshire*, but a dip in sales with the fourth book *Walking My Dog in East Yorkshire and Some of the Parts of North, South and West Yorkshire I Didn't Quite Get Around to Covering Before*, is persuaded by his publishers to buy a goat, solely so he can write a book about it. This is in preference to his early idea of buying a bird of prey and getting his family to teach it tricks, purely so he can write a memoir about it called *Our Kestrel Manoeuvres in the Dark*. Mayhem ensues, as he spends all of the advance he has received from his publishers on building a shed for the goat and goat-proofing his garden,

falls out with his editor, claiming it was all his fault, and then makes up with him, as they realise their arguments will contribute greatly to the narrative. Finally, while still having trouble with David's size and the fact that everyone who meets him claims he has 'Satan eyes', it looks like his fortunes will turn around when he meets Marissa, a spellbinding, earthy fortune teller of gypsy extraction. But they don't.

Size Matters

By the summer of 2011, I had developed an evening routine that probably wasn't dissimilar to that of many single men in their mid-thirties who live under the rule of cats. I spent a bit too much time watching epic HBO DVD box sets with my attention span compromised by Facebook, Twitter and text messages, stopping every now and then to rescue a vole inside an old coffee mug or gently remove a small set of jaws from my ankle (actually, maybe that wasn't something other single men in their thirties who lived with cats did; just single men in their thirties who lived with Shipley). I ate quite healthily, if a little lazily, piercing a few more film lids than I would want to admit. If I also spent a bit too much time talking to my pets, then at least I could reassure myself that it was better than talking to myself and that I had an active social life.

My most animated conversations were generally with Shipley and Ralph, neither of whom had ever quite understood that not everything in life has to have a soundtrack. I could have blamed myself for allowing their rowdiness to get out of control over the years, but sometimes, as I knew only too well from the time I had spent in the company of my dad, my granddad and my dad's uncle Ken, loudness runs in a family and there's nothing you can do about it. Volume was the common ground reminding you that Ralph and Shipley came from the same litter, on the occasions you wondered how it was possible for two cats to be related when they looked approximately as different to one another as an under-sized lion and a spider monkey.

An entrance was always cause for fanfare. Had either of them owned a small trumpet, I'm sure they would have sounded it when they came through the cat door. I hoped that, just once, when they rushed through it, meowing at the top of their voices, they might lead me to an injured animal or a child trapped down a well, but it never happened.

'RAAAAAAALPHHH!' Ralph would shout.

'Did that big crow say something derogatory about your sideburns again?' I would reply.

'RALLLRALLLRALLPH.'

'Don't worry. You're fine. The metal clothes horse isn't coming out today. All my laundry's completely up to date. And I promise that if I do wash my hands, I'll wait at least half an hour before I stroke you.'

'RAAAAAAALPHHH!'

'It's Obama, isn't it? You're wondering if he'll be the subject of a Republican smear campaign and not get in

for a second term. I've told you, it's too early to be worrying about that. We've still got the best part of a year
and a half, so just try to relax.'

'RAAAAAAAAAAAAAALLLLLOOOOOO.'

'Oh God. Don't tell me. You went for a long walk and
someone was playing a Lily Allen song in their kitchen
nearby with the windows open. I knew it. I'm sorry.
Nobody deserves that. I should have been more sympathetic.'

My conversations with Shipley were frequently more
caustic, particularly on his part. 'You shouldn't really say
stuff like that,' I'd remonstrate with him, as his heavy
mortar fire of cat swearwords began. 'It's very hurtful,
and some people are less thick-skinned than me.'

On that evening way back a decade ago, when Dee
and I and our friends Steve and Sue had collected Ralph
(who, at that point, before we'd been informed of his
gender by a reliable source, had been known as
'Prudence'), Brewer and Shipley from their original
home in Essex, Shipley had been the 'extra choice': the
cat Steve had called 'the ugly one who looks like Yoda',
but whom I'd been swayed into taking home by his
adorably awkward, runtish exuberance. That first night
Ralph and Brewer had curled up in the respective crooks
of my right arm and Dee's, but Shipley had slept quietly
alone at our feet, in an 'It's OK – I know my place!' sort
of way. As it turned out, though, he didn't know his
place at all, and had only been preserving his energy
before bursting into action the next day. Since then, the
backchat had rarely stopped, except on the occasions

when he was asleep or I turned him upside down. Even when I had parties, he could often be found in the centre of a group of my friends, disagreeing with them just for the sake of it, or making outlandish, boastful claims about his recent achievements.

If The Bear was the quietly beating heart of the household, and Ralph was its face, then Shipley was its notoriously volatile public relations man: its very own version of Malcolm Tucker from *The Thick of It*. Nothing got past him, and his adrenaline was a constant presence in my life. I was so used to gently removing his claws from my posterior when sitting at the computer in an open-backed chair, or stopping him climbing up my leg when I was near the fridge, I often didn't know I was doing it: each action had become just another humdrum, unconscious thing I did with one of my limbs, like sweeping my hair out of my face, or scratching behind one of my ears. While Ralph and The Bear seemed in completely different ways to be assured about their status as the most important cat in the house, with no need to boast about it, Shipley was on a constant self-publicity drive, keen to explain to everyone that he was the *real* important cat around here. He didn't seem to mind whether his audience was me, his furry housemates, my friends, a man who had come over to cut the ivy out of my boiler or a mallard who wandered into the conservatory one day by mistake.

There was never any malice to it. His uncouth behaviour always stopped short of nastiness, and that was why, despite their long-term animosity, I never got to the point of permanently splitting him and The Bear up. Turn Shipley upside down, and he was fine. Jiggling him about a bit helped, too. I'd never seen any animal, or human, able to go so quickly from petulance to docility. The only feline mood swing I'd seen come close to it was a few years ago when I'd offered Ralph a piece of left-over chicken balti then immediately washed my hands and assembled the metal clothes horse.

When I arrived home with heavy shopping bags, Shipley was invariably the first to greet me. Though I might be tired and desperate to eat, I followed the logic of all gullible idiots, putting my shopping bags to one side and feeding the cats first. If I'd bought bread, I knew I had to be quick getting the cat food into the bowls, as experience had taught me that the absolute maximum you could leave a sliced loaf unattended before Shipley would eat it was twenty-seven seconds. Had I placed a slice of bread in Shipley's food bowl, he would have sniffed at me in the manner of an ungrateful heiress who'd never known suffering, then walked away, but if the bread was packaged and ostensibly out of bounds on the kitchen counter, it was different. This was yet another example of the fact that cats don't just make haste for the Munchies taste, but for the sweet taste of nonconformism.

When the cat food itself was placed on the floor, Shipley tore through it at twice the speed of his peers, and – if I didn't stay vigilant – would swiftly move towards Ralph or The Bear, nudge them out of the way and start on theirs. I'd seen Ralph casually pummel

Shipley when his sleek black brother got out of hand in other situations, but when it came to dining matters, he was willing to move aside. Surely food was important to Ralph, as a cat approximately the size of a sports utility vehicle? Maybe it was, but clearly not so important as it was to Shipley, whose metabolism somehow managed to transform all that meaty sustenance into pure muscle: the kind that allowed him to be the only one of my cats who could force my bedroom door open in the middle of the night using his sheer wiry strength.

The Bear had a very different approach to mealtimes. When the other cats were around, he hung back, watchfully. He was the only feline I'd ever met who signalled his hunger not by cursing, meowing or using my leg as a scratching post, but by nodding subtly towards the food cupboard. He usually bided his time before doing this; having waited until the other cats were out tormenting a squirrel or vole, he would then quietly creep into the kitchen and catch me on my own. Bafflingly, he seemed to be able to distinguish, before the shopping bags were open, the times when I'd bought him turkey from those when I hadn't. His most vocal request, at times like this, would be a tiny, persuasive *meeoop* – never anything more.

Similarly, The Bear was always at his most affectionate and playful when there were no other cats around. He still wrestled with a five-year-old squeaky toy mouse far more enthusiastically than you'd expect from an old age pensioner, but if he thought another cat was watching him, he'd abruptly bring a halt to proceedings. The times

when he sat on my lap were rare; they involved a vast
amount of nervous circling for position, and only
occurred when Ralph and Shipley were well out of sight.
Since I'd been living on my own, I had worked my way
up to a point with Ralph where more or less all I had to
do to get him to sit on my lap was look at him with a
raised eyebrow. The Bear needed much more encouragement, but, once in position, there was no doubting his
commitment. I'd never known a cat to purr for more
lengthy, sustained periods. His purr had a high-pitched
quaver to it, as if, just as he seemed to experience hurt in
an exaggerated manner, he experienced happiness that
little bit more acutely than other cats. I also felt he was
trying to explain something to me. 'OK,' he seemed to be
saying. 'This is just a taste of how things could be, if you
ditched those two other losers. I'm leaving it up to you,
but to my mind there's only one way to go here. We're
both men of the world. Well, me more than you, *obviously*, but I think it's demeaning both of us to live with
creatures of lesser intelligence.'

It was during one of these intense one-on-one
moments with The Bear that, in July, I finally got a
proper look at Andrew. He'd been visiting ever more frequently, and was gradually working his way backwards
through my LP collection. I'd put all the albums in
protective polythene sleeves, but I was still very concerned: the Jimmy Webbs had already got it in a major
way and all the signs pointed to my original copy of Scott
Walker's seminal 1969 album, *Scott 4*, being next. More
troublingly still, I'd caught The Bear following his

example. It had been a while since The Bear had soiled anything indoors, and I'd forgotten just how hard it was to be angry with him when he did. As I watched him spraying a small jet of urine over Stevie Wonder's *Innervisions* and *Songs in the Key of Life*, he gave the nearest approximation of a carefree smile that I had ever seen on his features. I placed him firmly outside on the balcony, remonstrating 'This is beneath you, The Bear!' and attempting to reason with him in other ways I felt might appeal to his intellectual vanity, but within half an hour, he was back inside, eating cooked turkey out of my hand and doing his most ecstatic chirrup-purr.

As this exchange occurred, I could hear a loud munching from the corner where I kept the biscuit dispensers. I assumed that the animal making the noise was Ralph, who ate with the same slobbery gusto with which he snored and purred, so it was an even bigger surprise, a minute later, to see Andrew emerge from the alcove, stop dead in his tracks and stare straight at us. I was amazed at the softness and sweetness of his face up close. This was not the face of a predator or a thief. It was not even the face of an Andrew. It was a dreamy, moony face: the kind of face you wouldn't be surprised to find at twilight wandering in a daze around a foreign campsite, looking for its tent.

The stand-off between Andrew and The Bear and me only lasted twenty seconds, and concluded with our feral friend's usual balustrade-hurtling exit towards the cat-flap, but seeing him up close gave me hope for our future together – or his future living with my parents, at least.

Not only did there seem to be loving potential in his face, but I'd noticed scabs around his ears, more evidence that he was homeless.

Not that I had any shortage of new tenant offers elsewhere. Barely a week went by without someone offering me a cat to adopt, but I was determined to stand firm for the time being. Nor were the offers limited to the whiskery. After I'd visited an animal rescue centre in north Norfolk, Jane, a friend who volunteered there, offered me a pygmy goat to adopt. The idea was appealing, but I had to decline, having researched a) just how much different stuff goats like to eat, b) just how much of that stuff is poisonous to them, and c) just how much it would bankrupt me to make the garden goat-proof. I reasoned that if I couldn't afford a new roof and shed for myself then I probably couldn't afford them for a waist-high horned creature with a chequered past.

In another of my less pragmatic moments, I did seriously consider an alpaca. I even carried out some research into the matter, going trekking with a few of them in the company of Mary and Will – who, Mary was often heard to claim, 'looks a lot like an alpaca' – near Wells-next-the-Sea on the Norfolk coast. Alpacas originally hail from South America, and are part of the same camelid family that includes camels, llamas – the creature which, with the possible exception of Will, they most resemble – and guanacos. They differ from llamas in being smaller and more sheeplike, and in being bred primarily for their wool.

They're quite common in Britain now, yet a surprising

number of people are still unfamiliar with them. 'What's an alpaca?' asked a couple of friends, to whom I patiently explained that it was a character from the children's TV show *In the Night Garden* which had escaped and now lived wild, surviving on its wits. My mum was surprised when I explained to her that 'alpaca trekking' meant 'alpaca walking' and not 'alpaca riding', but even a seven-year-old child passenger would probably have proved too weighty for the six alpacas I met. Macchu, Picchu, Pedro, Costello, Padro and Pepe were all much daintier once you got close to them and realised just how much of their bulk was made up of fur.

I'd fancied alpaca or llama trekking for a few years, and not just because I felt it was the closest I might ever get to recreating the early scenes of *The Empire Strikes Back*. After an unsuccessful call to a local llama sanctuary, whose denizens were suffering from the viral ruminant disease blue tongue – an affliction I'd made the mistake of referring to in the recent past as both 'blue tooth' and 'camel toe' – my search had led me to Ian, a sleepily cheerful man in late middle age with a sun-blasted face that spoke of the happiest kind of north Norfolk life. Ian booked me, Will and Mary in for a two-hour trek with his fleet of charismatic alpacas. It turned into something very close to what Will repeatedly described as 'The best day ever!' but then if I was being honest I'd suspected it wouldn't be anything less, right from the moment Ian had answered my opening question, 'Is now a good time to talk?' with the statement 'Well, I have hold of six alpacas and a cheese sandwich, but, yes, it's fine.'

'These are runt alpacas,' explained Ian when we arrived. 'They're the ones none of the breeders want.' Because of this, each of his Peruvian and Chilean alpacas had cost him only a few hundred pounds and were, he said, 'very cheap to run', surviving mainly on grass and chopped apples. One thing alpacas don't like – as Ian informed us, just after I'd looked directly into Macchu's eyes – was being looked directly in the eyes. I noted this down, thinking of the irreconcilable problems it might cause for The Bear.

The other thing about alpacas is that they fart. A lot. Fart, in fact, in the manner of animals who have found out that farting is to be outlawed in only a few sweet hours. In this sense, I'd drawn the long straw by being at the head of the party with Macchu, leaving it to Mary, directly behind me with Picchu, to bear the brunt of his refried grass smells. Macchu was, Ian told me, quite the drama queen, known to get in a bit of a flap around dogs and swift-limbed humans, and – atypically for an animal whose DNA had been shaped by mountainous terrain – a bit unsure of himself on slopes. 'He once fell down a steep grassy bank,' said Ian. 'And early on when I started walking him, he'd often sit down in a middle of a trek and refuse to move.' That Macchu was the organically elected leader of the group was a measure of the intriguingly inverted manner in which alpacas sort out their power struggles. Here, weak and nervy men were to be looked up to and admired. It was an intriguing state of affairs, and you couldn't help but dwell for a moment on what might happen if the alpaca hierarchical system was transposed to the human universe: Private Godfrey from *Dad's Army* being sent up in a fighter plane above enemy skies, say, or Woody Allen finding himself selected for a dangerous polar mission.

As a treat, towards the end of the trek the alpacas were led towards a sandy stretch of bridleway near the coast road, where they could enjoy a dust bath before chowing down on the chopped apples that Will, Mary and I had been instructed to bring for them. I could tell that Macchu was looking forward to at least one of these events because from about the three-quarter mark of the trek he'd been making an odd quivering sound in the back of his throat, not unlike The Bear's chirrup-purr. As someone whose favourite member of the Muppets is Beaker, I didn't mind being with a creature of such comically jumpy disposition, but I did look across enviously from time to time at Will and Mary's more mellow alpacas – particularly Will's charge, Pedro, whose impressive fringe I would later find myself trying to mimic in the rear-view mirror of the car while stopped at some traffic lights just outside Fakenham.

Perhaps in retaliation for me staring him out earlier, Macchu, having wolfed down the apples, chose to shower some of them right back in my face. I was told by Ian that, in alpaca world, such an enthusiastic flob is seen as 'a gesture of affection'. Nor was it entirely unpleasant. Alhough, slightly less pleasantly, I was still finding bits of congealed Granny Smith-flavoured saliva in my beard and hair an hour later.

While my adventures in the Norfolk countryside tempted me to expand and diversify my crew of animal lodgers, they also showed me the commitment I would need to do so responsibly. Never was this more apparent than when I visited Karen, a friend who, with her husband Jeff, maintained her own smallholding and free-range food company a couple of miles up the road. 'Here are my jobs, and that's just for this morning,' Karen said, holding up a sheet of A4 entirely covered in text on both sides, as we sat in her kitchen. I'd been very busy the previous day, but her list made my own, written on my kitchen blackboard – now half crossed out and shot through with a derisory dribble of Andrew's urine – look rather shameful.

Below us on the floor, one of her Siamese cats, Vinnie, dragged an old, saliva-sodden toy rabbit, which was missing one of its legs, over to his food bowl and began to eat. 'He always does that,' said Karen. 'He doesn't seem to enjoy his food as much unless it's by his side. It was an old toy cat before that – a pathetic thing that looked as if it was crippled – but that's now interred in the new kitchen wall we built. If he can't find the rabbit, he'll usually substitute it with a slipper.' In addition to their cats, Jeff and Karen lived with sheep, dogs, a rather magnificently attired fop scarecrow, and several varieties of pigs and chickens; the latter included a frizzled Poland called Colonel Fitzwilliam, who Karen described as 'a right bugger' and who bobbed about feistily behind the wire mesh of his run as I greeted him, not unlike a striker in a football match jostling for position amongst an imaginary opposing team's defence in anticipation of a corner.

Fitzwilliam was, however, less formidable than The General, the cockerel Jeff and Karen had owned back when they founded their Samphire food company. The General had a dislike of the colour red that could be considered extreme even in the notoriously red-hating cockerel universe, and had once viciously cornered a man who had come to clean their kitchen Aga. Apparently The General 'didn't take kindly to the big red face on his Henry vacuum cleaner'.

Karen had been particularly keen to show me a couple of her new lambs, Grayling, who she described as 'the boldest lamb I have ever met', and his much smaller brother Thomas, who was hypothermic when he was born and had to live in Karen's living room for a while. Karen is a person who will make the statement 'There's a lamb in my living room' in much the same way other people say 'There are some apples in my kitchen'.

When Karen wants her sheep to come to her, she shouts 'Sheep!' at them. I watched her do this and the bounding, woolly results were joyful to witness, inspiring in me hope for the obedience of all sorts of undomesticated animals: the belief that, to finally achieve their often overlooked cuddly potential, ultimately all a Mediterranean seaside cave full of lizards might need was a little love and a kind, outdoorsy woman to shout

'Lizards!' at them every day. I'd recently made the tentative decision to go vegetarian, and I'd felt bashful about visiting Karen and Jeff: not only did I know I'd have to admit to them that I could no longer eat their delicious pork pies, but I would have to get my head out of the sand and stare what I'd been eating in its adorable, fluffy face – even, as it turned out in Grayling's case, to massage that same fluffy face and let it nibble a considerable portion of my trousers.

I felt more philosophical than I'd imagined, meeting Grayling and his friends. The Samphire animals were hugely loved, and the ethical difference between eating them and being a veggie seemed far less vast than, say, that between eating them and eating the hens that I saw cramped into the disgusting-smelling lorries that regularly barrelled past my house on the way to the local chicken factory. All the same, I doubted my ability to take on even a minor version of Karen and Jeff's workload. 'There's never really a time when I'm off duty,' said Karen. 'When you take this lifestyle on, you accept that you don't go on holiday.'

My reservations about making such a commitment were reinforced when, on a walk near the village of Garboldisham, I was enlisted to rescue an escaped turkey by another smallholding owner, Georgie, who was just returning to her land. I'd been doing some research on ancient burial mounds for something I was writing that week, and my intention at the beginning of the afternoon had been to find the barrow allegedly containing the two-thousand-year-old remains of the rebel Iceni

Queen Boudicca. Instead I ended up spending a couple of serendipitous hours meeting the livestock owned by Georgie and her husband Richard, and riding on the back of Richard's tractor to go onion picking. The escaped turkey turned out to be fine and when Georgie let me hold it, I amazed myself by doing so without shouting 'Bollocks! It's a massive live turkey! In my actual arms!' But as it struggled and clucked in my grasp, I noticed another turkey in the field behind us, limping along in an extremely sorry fashion.

'Is that one OK?' I asked her.

'I don't think so,' she replied. 'One of the others probably jumped on its back, and we might have to put it out of its misery.'

When you keep animals – big, proper, messy outdoor animals that you can potentially get very attached to – this is everyday life. I'm sure you become slightly numbed by it after a while. But what if you don't *want* to become numbed by it?

It all brought me back, once again, to cats. I'd done pretty well with my three. Each of them clearly thought I was OK, despite the fact that I was from a vastly inferior species to them; none of them required me to muck them out, or regularly call a vet to my property to see to their various ailments. For a terminally soppy person like me, who enjoyed country life but still wanted to have a life outside it, they were the perfect pets. I refused to put them in a cattery, on the basis that they had no way of knowing I was ever coming back for them, and I rarely left them alone for long, but at least I still let myself have some kind of existence beyond them. Were I to have a couple of goats or pigs, that would be The End. I would be tied to their every need, and would never stay a night away from home again. I would end up being defined as a Goat Person or a Pig Person far more than I had ever allowed myself to be defined as a Cat Person.

I'd travelled very little in the last few years. Partly I'd been unable to afford holidays, and partly I'd had a wussy reluctance to leave my cats. But this summer I had at least managed to make a few brief trips to the other side of the country. Sticking to my usual habit of doing things in the most difficult way possible, I had decided that 2011 would be the year when I fell in love with someone who lived 367 miles away. I was introduced to Gemma by a friend of a friend, and it had taken us a whole half-hour of our first face-to-face meeting to decide that we wanted to be together, despite the fact that she resided in deepest, darkest Devon and I lived in lightest Norfolk.

It could not have become much clearer during our early conversations that she was a fellow animal nut. It came as no surprise to me when she confessed she was marginally more of a Dog Person than a Cat Person, but she loved cats too. In fact she had, until very recently, been living with one – an animal who, judging from her exclamations of pain during our early phone conversations, spent a large portion of its time using her as a climbing frame. When she was younger, she'd had the pleasure of cuddling a lion cub, and on one of our first country walks together, she'd also informed me that she'd 'milked loads of stuff' – a statement whose initially cloudy nature was clarified when she added that her primary school had been located on a farm. She was also the first person I'd ever dated who had picked up a real live Emperor penguin in her arms and cuddled it. 'They're not as rubbery as you think,' she explained.

Gemma was briefly back living with her parents and, before we visited their house, she warned me that their rescue dog, a Jack Russell/terrier cross called Scrumpy, had an aversion to men with beards. 'We think he was used for fighting before we got him from the rescue centre,' she explained. 'Our theory is that one of the men who made him do it had a lot of facial hair, and he wants revenge,' she continued, as I involuntarily put a protective hand up to the thick fuzz on my cheeks and chin. Our initial encounter reminded me of the time in 1997 that I'd emerged out of Glasgow Central station and immediately been asked for a fight by a small, wiry Scotsman wielding a can of Kestrel super-strength lager. I sensed it was less that Scrumpy didn't approve of my beard; more that he would like to eat it, preferably accompanied by a side order of face. In time, though, I won him over, even being permitted to tickle his stomach on my third visit. 'He can never meet your cats, though,' said Gemma. 'He *hates* cats.'

Before her first visit to my house, I briefed Gemma thoroughly about The Bear. I knew his intensity could come as a shock to the uninitiated. When she arrived, the cats filed out to meet her in the order I'd anticipated: Shipley arriving first, to show her around the place and explain the various improvements he'd made to it recently, followed by Ralph, a little nervously at first, but soon permitting her to revel in his magnificent sideburns.

'Why does he keep doing that squinting face?' Gemma asked.

'Have you washed your hands recently?' I said.

'Yes, I did it as soon as we got in.'

'That'll be it, then. He can't stand that. He'll be better in half an hour or so, when the skin's natural oils start to return.'

'Raaaaaaalph!' said Ralph.

Twenty minutes later, The Bear arrived. I say 'arrived'; it was actually more like he materialised. It had been raining, and, without warning, there he was not three feet away from where we sat, drenched, wide-eyed and glistening, in a ray of fresh sunlight that seemed to be shining just for him – seemed, even, to be what had transported him here – peering at us as if looking simultaneously into Gemma's past and our future. In so many situations, The Bear eschewed the vulgarities of everyday feline behaviour, but he had the same reaction to rain as my other cats: it seemed to imbue him with extra confidence. Mostly the confidence to find a human and wipe the rain on them as quickly as possible. As he went about his work of using various parts of me as a towel, his eyes burned into Gemma.

'I feel like he knows all my secrets,' she said.

'Oh, I'm sure he does by now,' I said. 'He's obviously not too upset by them. Otherwise he'd have been out of here by now.'

'I can't believe he's a cat. It's like there's a little person in there, behind his eyes.'

She reached beneath The Bear's chin to give him a scrumble, and he accepted it. He then made one of his rare forays onto my lap, and began his gradual, meticulous routine of getting settled.

'Why does he keep going round and round like that?' asked Gemma.

'That's just his ritual. This is nothing. Sometimes he'll do it sixteen or seventeen times before he finally plonks himself down. His all-time record is thirty-six.'

'Oh, I see.'

'It's good that you seem to get on, because when we split up, he'll be yours.'

'How do you mean?'

'That's just the way it works.'

In the evening, the final furry member of the household arrived, his stealth in creeping through the cat door too quiet for his entrance to be audible, although his heft on the conservatory roof had given him away a couple of minutes before that. 'Be very quiet,' I told Gemma, as we crept up the stairs and poked our heads around the corner to see Andrew munching from the biscuit dispenser.

'Oh, he's beautiful,' whispered Gemma. 'He definitely doesn't look like an Andrew to me, though. Much more like a Sven, I reckon.'

'Hmm. You could be right. But isn't he a bit too big for Sven? I think of Svens as being quite fitness-conscious.'

Andrew-Sven was looking a bit chubbier of late, which didn't surprise me. Since his visits had increased, my cat food bills had too, by no small amount. I also had to bear in mind that, even when you were buying in bulk, the cost of replacement protective polythene sleeves for records could mount up. I found myself torn: on one hand, I wanted to get to know him and find out what made him tick, and I wanted my mum to have a cat. On the other hand, I still wanted to be able to afford to feed myself. As usual, though, the side of the scales weighted towards feline needs seemed to be triumphing.

Later that night, I woke to the sound of Gemma wheezing next to me. Her mum was severely allergic to cats, but she'd never previously had a problem herself, and had lived with at least one cat for most of the last six years. It made no sense, but in another way it made complete sense: the reinstatement of the old clause in my romantic life stating that I could only be properly attracted to women who either didn't like, or were physically incompatible with, cats. We opened more windows, and Gemma huffed on her asthma inhaler, but it was no help.

The following night she found herself in a similarly breathless, uncomfortable state. Then I noticed an odd thing: Gemma was also wheezing slightly when she sat on the sofa in the living room, but seemed completely fine when she was upstairs in the kitchen. The sofa cushions were filled with goose down, just like my duvet. That night I swapped the latter for the synthetic duvet from the spare bedroom and mercifully Gemma's respiratory problems were no more.

'I'm so relieved,' she said. 'I don't want to be allergic to The Bear. How can anyone be allergic to The Bear? He's The Bear!'

The two of them had already formed a significant bond. Being from a working-class background and a natural worrier, Gemma ticked two of his biggest boxes. The fact that she liked the music of sensitive, melancholic singer-songwriters, rather than the overblown seventies rock and power ballads I was partial to, almost certainly helped, too.

'Does he always follow you around like that, staring at you?' she asked.

'Almost always,' I said.

It was true that The Bear had been more reluctant than ever to let me out of his sight in the last few months. I'd got to know a fair bit about black cats in the last decade – about that certain kind of intensity and magic they often seem to have, which other cats don't – but being followed around like this by one without quite knowing what it meant had a way of making me feel a bit like Britain's most useless witch. In many of the pictures I took of my other cats during this period, The Bear was often there, in the background, stealing the limelight with his own kind of photobomb, all based on magnetic soulfulness rather than bolshy physical one-upmanship. If he had an anthem for his twilight years, it would have been 'Alone' by Heart. I was aware that I was overly partial to anthropomorphism and I knew that when he *did* get me alone, much of his agenda was about cooked meat, but it wasn't as if his gaze diminished in purpose when his appetite was satisfied. It *had* to be about more than that. Had he been stalking me in order to ask, 'So if God is nice, why do children get ill and are men always at war?' or, 'So if so many people love the music of Nick Drake, why did he die depressed and unappreciated at the tender age of just 122 cat years?' I could not have felt his sweet, beseeching bewilderment more acutely. When you added the fact that the customary camp wobble in his walk as he followed me was more of an arthritic wobble now, the daily heartbreak was only exaggerated.

Whenever I went to visit Gemma, I felt slightly guilty. Not only was I leaving The Bear, whose habit was to sulk in the aftermath of any slightly prolonged period I spent away from home, I was foisting his melancholy on Deborah and David, who had kindly and innocently offered to feed him, Shipley and Ralph. But, having known him for a while, they were getting used to it, and I even felt I was doing The Bear a favour. There was always the chance they could put a word in for him with their ageing cat Biscuit, for whom he seemed to hold a candle even after seven years of stony rejection.

I remembered, a decade earlier, talking through the routine of cat feeding to Bob, my first ever next door neighbour as a home owner, and feeling very adult as I did so. 'The kettle's just here,' I'd announced, 'and feel free to have a sit-down and watch TV if you like.' It only occurred to me later what a ridiculous thing it had been to say. Why on earth would Bob, a retired headmaster, want to have a cup of tea and watch TV in a virtual stranger's house instead of his own, sixteen yards away? But suggesting such a thing to Deborah and David wouldn't have been quite so preposterous. Not only were they happy to feed the cats, they were also happy to stick around and give them a cuddle, particularly Shipley, whose relationship with Deborah continued to be close – if somewhat foul-mouthed, on Shipley's side.

After one visit to Devon I returned to find each of my cats' names, and Biscuit's, written on the kitchen blackboard, alongside an arcane set of measurements. I puzzled over these for a while. I knew Biscuit was a small cat, but I was sure she must be more than seven inches long. Only after an hour did I have a lightbulb moment and realise that the figures related to the cats' tails. It said a lot about Ralph and Shipley's relationship that Shipley's pointy, slightly curly tail, even though it looked the longest, was actually only runner-up; coming in at ten and a half inches, it was a full half-inch behind Ralph's. That said, I would not have put it past Ralph to add a bit of length with some crafty backcombing. I hoped it would not intensify The Bear's aura of melancholy that his came in second last, at nine inches. Shipley would probably be most troubled by the measurements, and this was arguably confirmed when I found him next to the blackboard, his tail in the air, seemingly trying to straighten out the kink at the end of it.

One day in November, heading inland to pick Gemma up from her day job in her dad's shop, feeling battered and windswept from a rainy early-morning walk on a remote stretch of Devon coast, I found an answerphone message from Deborah. 'I'm sorry to bother you,' she said. 'But it's Shipley. He's been refusing to eat for the last day, and seems very lethargic. Every time I go to check on him, he's just sitting on the beanbag in the same position, and he barely reacts when I touch him.'

Finding themselves in a situation that all pet sitters dread, Deborah and David had faced a difficult decision. Considerately, they hadn't wanted to worry me when I was so far from home, but they'd also not wanted to leave matters too late. After I'd called Deborah back and talked it through, she and David kindly rushed Shipley to see George, the Californian vet down the road, who seemed rather stumped as to exactly what the matter was, but gave him an injection of antibiotics, and said he should be brought back the following day if there'd been no improvement in his condition.

Later that afternoon, I called Deborah back to find out if Shipley had improved. 'There's no change,' she said. 'I've been sitting with him, but he seems very limp and sad. He's not even swearing at me.' With seven counties separating us, Gemma working two jobs, and my own weekly writing commitments to consider, it had already been difficult for Gemma and me to find time to see each other as much as we wanted to. Now here I was, doing the only thing I could do in the situation, and leaving, not much more than a day after I'd arrived.

I raced back across the country in record time, incurring a speeding ticket along the way at a time in my life when I had never had less use for one, and only stopping to fill up on petrol and read a couple of text message updates from Deborah. When I arrived home, Shipley was lying on his beanbag: the same one he'd been on nine months previously when I'd found Janet slumped on the stairs. Usually, if I arrived back after even a few hours out of the house he'd be the first cat to greet me, getting right up in my face to tell me exactly how I'd let him down and list the gifts he now required as compensation, but now he barely raised his chin as I arrived in the room. When I scrumbled him underneath it and gave the top of his head a scritch, there were none of his usual attempts to push his nose – usually so cold, now so dry and warm – into my knuckle, or engineer a way to get the same knuckle or a finger under the side of his lip (always a weird habit of his and Ralph's: another subtle family trait). His sinewy limbs felt lifeless, and he put up little resistance as I transferred him to a wicker cat igloo that – like most purpose-built cat beds – he'd always disliked. The Bear watched all this, perhaps confused at the new domestic arrangement where he could walk around freely, without anyone dancing about in front of his face and swearing.

I called George the vet on the emergency number and we agreed that the best thing I could do was bring Shipley over again first thing in the morning. Shipley – a cat who would so often force open the bedroom door, and was normally so desperate to make the room his – now seemed indifferent to the rare privilege of being its sole feline occupant. I probably would have slept fitfully anyway, as I usually did after the drive from Devon to Norfolk, but I woke at regular intervals throughout the night, reaching out every half-hour to his igloo, to touch his flank and make sure he was still breathing. If that sounds overdramatic, it was done from the perspective of someone who'd only six months ago received a stark lesson about the gossamer thread that separates feline life from death.

All my cats, past and present, had different ways of reacting to a trip to the vet's. Pablo's check-ups had been soundtracked by a bloodcurdling war cry that didn't let up from the moment I started the car to the moment he was unloaded onto the examining table – possibly to signal his fear that he was being transported back to the harsh feral world he had come from. At the other end of the scale, Ralph would act like he was far too fancy for the whole fiasco, then undermine himself by eating one of his scabs in front of the vet, or letting off a fart of the variety known at my secondary school as 'silent but violent'. Bootsy had always largely seen it as another opportunity to be admired by strangers. Janet had weathered the experience with faintly wounded stoicism, and The Bear gave the impression of plotting darkly in the back of his cat basket, while periodically lamenting his existential condition with his broken-smoke-alarm *meeoop*. With Shipley, it was expletives all the way, combined with the hint of a sense that, given half the chance, he would be up and out of his basket to take on any Jack Russell, Rottweiler or giant lop-eared rabbit who happened to be in the waiting room at the time, possibly with one paw strapped behind his back.

Today was different. That he did not utter a single profanity at me from the moment I ushered him into his basket to the moment George began to examine him was perhaps the plainest measure of how poorly he was.

I was amazed at how much weight he seemed to have lost in just a couple of days of not eating. George still seemed baffled by his condition, but gave him a series of antibiotics. 'We'll give him the works, and see if it helps,' he said. 'These will take a while before they have any effect. The best thing might be for you to go out for a little while, take your mind off it, then see how he is, and give us a call if there's no improvement.'

As instructed, having placed Shipley on the bed, with a plate of turkey chunks easily within reach, I left the house, striding deep into the Norfolk countryside: so often my saviour in times of trouble. As I walked, I thought about all the times I'd said mean things about Shipley to my friends – the occasion last week, for example, when Katia had asked after his well-being, and I'd described him as 'a crocodile-faced thug'. I thought about the cats' mealtimes, when I would purposely put his food out last. This was a mandatory measure, due to the speed and greed with which Shipley ate, but I still felt bad about it. Had I ever singled Shipley out for a special turkey treat while the other cats were asleep, in the way I did with The Bear? A few times, but maybe not enough. Because Shipley was so demanding, so completely, constantly in your face, there never appeared to be any need to make sure he got enough attention. But there was nothing to say he wasn't just like Ralph and The Bear: nurturing his own little dream of being my only cat. Perhaps even more so, in a way. Maybe Shipley's attacks on The Bear came about because he heard what I said about The Bear – my comments about how intellectual and gentle and special he was – and felt lonely and neglected. During my last relationship I'd always been the one who saw the good in Shipley, but maybe I hadn't been seeing enough good in him. He was still the same kitten who'd waited at the end of the bed that night in 2001: wanting to be close to the action, and thinking of ways to get there, ahead of the prettier or more intellectual cats.

'He's an amazing cat,' Gemma had told me. 'I've never known a cat like this, who's so patient when you wobble him about and stuff. I mean, I know he comes across like a bit of a hooligan at first, but he never seems to go off in a huff, like other cats.'

Shipley's default mode might have been 'potential ASBO', but when you were actually giving him attention, no cat could match him for tolerance. If Ralph was sleeping on my chest and I adjusted position, he'd usually storm out of the room, like a rock star waltzing off stage in a tantrum because the sound man hadn't quite got the level of his vocals correct. If I did the same thing while Shipley was sleeping on or near me, he didn't mind, as long as I was planning to stick around. There was none of the finessing you had to do with other cats; he wanted you to stroke him, ruffle him, jiggle him and turn him upside down, and he wanted you to do it as vigorously as possible. Or, to put it slightly differently, in the words of a friend who'd been massaging his neck at one of my parties: 'Essentially, he's a massive sado-masochistic perv.' Shipley was so muscular and strong and resilient, and there was so little sadness about his demeanour, you never stopped to consider that he could ever be frail or ill. But his body was vulnerable to the same diseases, the same chance mishaps, as any other cat. Something had invaded his system, or had misfired, or broken for good, and all that invincible boisterousness I'd taken for granted suddenly seemed impossibly fragile.

In the last two and a half years, I'd been repeatedly told by friends that I'd 'done well to hold it together', considering I'd been through a divorce, paid a large sum to buy someone out of a mortgage, and had to significantly rethink my future. But a lot of the things holding my life together still seemed very brittle: my ailing house, the fact that I was earning less than half of what I'd once earned and spending much of that on sustaining a new, long-distance relationship. I had doubts about how well I might cope if another of my cats died: another cat whose history was inexorably intertwined with a part of my life that I'd had to abandon.

Returning from my walk, I opened the front door with a lump in my chest. The house seemed eerily quiet. Ralph was out, and The Bear stood at the top of the stairs, as if he'd been waiting for me. 'I intuitively know everything you've been thinking,' said his eyes, 'and I've got various responses, but I think it's best if I put them in writing.' Shipley was on the bed, just where he'd been before, but as I entered the room, he stood up. He seemed wobbly, and it took him a couple of goes, but he was soon on his feet, and a small, throaty noise emerged from him. I couldn't make it out at first, but I leaned in more closely and asked him to repeat it.

'You're a dickhead,' he said.

'Pardon?' I said.

'You're a dickhead,' he repeated. 'Actually, no. A total nobhead. I'd kick your arse if I was twice as big as I am and didn't have this headache. Now pick me up and turn me upside down.'

I did what he requested, and heard, just perceptibly, the beginnings of a purr.

By that evening, Shipley was swearing again with alacrity. He swore at me, he swore at The Bear, he swore at Ralph; he swore, in a more affectionate way, at the turkey chunks I fed him. He even swore at a leaflet I'd brought home for Barometer World museum in the Devon town of Okehampton. I called Gemma to report the good news, but before I did so, I let Deborah know: she'd been texting every hour for a report on Shipley's condition, and was massively relieved. He was still a little wobbly, and didn't quite eat as much as usual, but whatever had been in George the vet's magic syringes seemed to have worked.

His reaction to being singled out for special treats, away from the others, and being allowed to sleep in my bedroom for a second night on the trot was much like what I imagine to be the reaction of a warlord who invades a new country and, instead of facing resistance, is greeted with open arms. He seemed a bit suspicious. However, he was soon taking full advantage of the latter privilege, purring aggressively in my face, inserting his bottom directly in front of the book of Alice Munro stories I was trying to read, and waking me up at 4 a.m. by pinching the skin on my elbow between his front teeth. I took all this – and the bagel he bit into the following morning while my back was turned – to mean he was on the mend.

Some Anonymous Cats I Have Psychoanalysed on my Travels (2010–2012)

Dustbathing flirt cat (Castle Acre, Norfolk, December 2010)

Probable name: Desdemona

Notes: Met subject on hill leading back into village after long walk. Was extremely tired, so couldn't actually be bothered to stroke subject, but subject refused to take no for an answer (abandonment issues?). Subject seems remarkably clean for one who patently enjoys rolling in dirt. Infer from this a possible tendency to overgroom as way of correcting mistakes subject feels it has made, and views as 'unclean'. Ultimately found it quite hard to leave subject behind, despite severely aching blisters and desperate need for large ale.

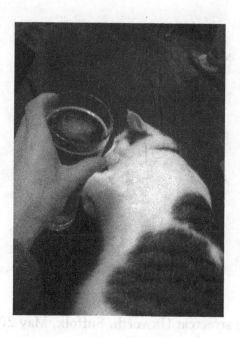

Pub cat (Norwich, February 2011)

Probable name: Albert

Notes: Sensed subject as easygoing presence, but instincts were wrong. Subject seemed irritable that I had taken its seat and when my friend Amy told subject that subject was 'magnificent', subject looked disdainful and let out small hiss. Subject clearly suffering from superiority complex, due to being fussed by punters all day. Could perhaps do with exposure to sparser environment, where people are not saying stuff like 'Wow! A cat! In a pub!' every five minutes, and take feline presence as more of a given.

Prowling streetcat (Ixworth, Suffolk, May 2011)

Probable name: Derek Blackshaw
Notes: Subject seems very comfortable in his habitat, though perhaps yearns to 'off road' in far flung places,

such as copse about five hundred yards away. Some complacency shown by culprit about living in cul-de-sac, perhaps contributing to subject's view of itself as 'well-to-do' and having 'made it in life'. However, subject seems confident yet not cocky. Had to try very hard not to take subject home, or at least not to take subject on walk to nearby village of Fornham St Martin.

Holiday cottage cat (Dartmoor, January 2012)

Probable name: Beryl
Notes: Subject immediately very friendly, willingly receiving chin scritches and bedding down on stomach. Subject has love of warmth, is enamoured – in a slightly weird druggy way – with log smells and is very sociable, no doubt

aided by coexisting every day with other cats and ducks, the latter of which subject seems to view in an impressively 'live and let live' fashion. Subject seemed genuinely friendly with both therapist and therapist's girlfriend, suggesting lasting psychological connection had occurred. However, look through guest book at comments such as 'I have never known a cat to be so friendly – it almost came home with us' and 'The in-house feline rocks!' suggests subject could suffer from debilitating commitment issues.

Weird car-watching cow cat (Golden Triangle area, Norwich, July 2012)

Probable name: John the Weird Car-Watching Cow Cat

Notes: Subject found on road, not far from house of Jay and Elizabeth, for whose party therapist was already late. Subject spent entire six minutes of session obsessively watching vehicles and refusing to answer therapist's queries. Subject exhibits signs of 'fake traffic warden syndrome', displacement issues and general truculence. Left subject to get on with own business with parting shot of 'OK: be like that, then'.

Magical wall cat (Covehithe, Suffolk, July 2012)

Probable name: Gwen
Notes: Subject seems very calm, despite threat to its home from extreme coastal erosion. Subject appeared to

prefer therapist's girlfriend, though exuded an amazing aura of peace that had profound effect on therapist too, and made therapist and girlfriend agree 'we want a cat just like this'. Upon leaving, therapist ended up waving to subject from car window, in very unprofessional and somewhat asinine manner.

Charity Begins at Home

Most adults will be familiar with the concept of Baby Fever: a concentrated, almost delirious period when, amongst your friends, breeding stops being merely co-incidental and becomes downright infectious. The concept of Kitten Fever is less widely documented, but equally common and possibly no less hysterical. I've known three or four notable periods of Kitten Fever in my life – even been swept up in one myself, around about 2001, leading to the adoption of Shipley, Ralph and Brewer – but probably none quite like the closing weeks of 2011. Between November and January, it seemed that everyone I knew was adopting a new ball of fur, and that *their* ball of fur was the most adorable, the most quirky, the most magical.

People who know I write about cats often make the mistake of assuming that my friends are a vast network of cat-mad people, that we all get one another's cats together each weekend for play dates involving balls of

wool and screenings of *Bagpuss*. For a prolonged period
in early 2009, a complete stranger – someone who'd read
about my books, but not read them – sent me regular
emails, asking me to set her up on a date with 'one of my
cat man mates', even though I'd replied to her initial
missive to say I only had three male friends at the time
who were huge cat lovers, and all of them were mar-
ried.* In truth, around half of my friends merely think
cats are 'sort of OK'. But in late 2001, even the cat-indif-
ferent amongst my acquaintances seemed to have come
around to the feline way of thinking. 'Do yours ever do
that thing where they run up the curtains?' said Ben,
who just six months ago had claimed to me in the pub
that cats were 'sort of selfish' and he didn't get on with
them, but now was enraptured with his new tortoiseshell
kitten. 'Bonzo does it, and it's amazing!'

'We seem to have a new cat,' Deborah announced.
'We think he's feral, and he's not always around, but he
seems to have taken a shine us. Have you seen him at
all?'

'What colour is he?' I asked.

'Ginger.'

'Oh. You mean Andrew!'

'No, this is definitely not Andrew. I've met Andrew
and never been able to get close to him. This one's very
friendly.'

A little before Christmas Gemma and I drove to the

* Each email featured an attachment containing a poem about one
of her cats.

Midlands, where we visited my dad and mum, whose relationship with Casper the friendly ghost cat – now a fully grown, proud specimen of cathood, and even more reminiscent of Monty – had reached an intimacy that had started to include grooming. (I hasten to add that the grooming was entirely carried out by my mum; Casper, being of noble stock, would never stoop to a job in the beauty industry.) 'YOUR MUM LOVES THAT CAT MORE THAN ME,' said my dad, emerging to greet us in the drive, having dragged himself away from the compost heap where he'd been having an afternoon nap.

On the way we visited my old friend Lucy, whose new cat Baldrick, a Ralphesque tabby with a giant tail that seemed to be held permanently perpendicular to the rest of his body, was proving to be a handful. 'He eats everything,' explained Lucy, stroking the huge Baldrick, who was the nearest I'd ever seen to a genetic experiment in which a cat has been crossed with one of the bendy buses introduced to the London transport network a few years ago. Yesterday, he had even eaten some of her decorative tinsel. 'I woke up this morning to a Christmas miracle in the litter tray: the year's first golden festive poo.' Baldrick did have his uses, though. Lucy had long complained that her housemate, Gary, had a disagreeable habit of walking around the place in ill-fitting trousers that displayed a considerable portion of his bottom. Last week, sitting on a backless chair, Gary had received something of a shock when Baldrick walked past beneath him, tail typically erect. 'It went, you know, *right into the crevice*,' said Lucy. 'He screamed quite loud. He's been a lot better at covering up ever since.'

Something about Baldrick's rather fetid youthful exuberance took me back wistfully to the younger days of Janet and Ralph. Not that I had any real need for another, younger vulgar cat. Ralph's gestures of vulgarity retained their erstwhile exuberance. Notable recent transgressions included cleaning his bottom at such a volume that I had to ask the man from the *Financial Times* I was speaking to on the telephone to repeat his email address three times, coming in through the cat door with algae stuck to his back legs, and coughing up a hairball of such formidable size, I felt I was being a little rude by not offering it a spare futon for the night. That said, Kitten Fever was having an undeniable effect on Gemma and me. We'd been together for a few months now, and knew that we could not carry on living on opposite sides of the country indefinitely. Speculation about a new cat of our own was inevitable.

'I had another dream about Chip last night,' Gemma told me. 'He was being a bit of an idiot, pushing his weight around. He brought in a frog.'

'Again?' I asked.

'Yep. Third time this week.'

By this point, I was very aware of Chip's habits and foibles: the obsession with amphibians and heights, his excessive moulting and frequent fights with other neighbourhood cats. This was fairly remarkable, considering there was a strong possibility that he was yet even to be born. It was the first time I'd ever had a girlfriend who'd mapped out a cat's personality before we'd met him, but I found myself getting swept away by the Chip legend, caught up in his mischievous yet intoxicating persona. The one problem I had with him was the moniker. To me Chip sounded like the name of a spoilt teenager from a 1980s American high school: the kind of kid who lorded it around the school, but was ultimately destined for a future of bar jobs and petty crime. I'd also kind of had my heart set on calling my next cat either F Cat Fitzgerald or Ethelbert – my favourite name for an Anglo-Saxon king, since it's the only one that contains an entire middle-aged couple from early 1960s Britain.

'No, no,' said Gemma. 'I mean Chip as in "potato". I hadn't thought about the American name. Are Americans really named that?'

'Yeah, I think it's what kids named Charles get called when they grow bigger and develop an irksome personality.'

'Oh, OK. That's not how I think of Chip at all.'

'What colour is he?'

'I told you: he's ginger, all over.'

This had become potentially overwhelming. If what Deborah said was to be believed, we already had two ginger cats in very close proximity to us. Bringing another into the mix – particularly one with a reputation for high jinks – could well turn out to be a mistake. Not that I had anything against gingers. Most of those I'd met had been sunny, upbeat sorts. Jackie, my ginger cat expert friend from Wales, once described them to me as 'Buddhists, living in the now' – a statement that made perfect sense when I first heard it, although later, when I thought more about it, I wondered what it said about Jackie's findings with regard to other cats. Had she discovered black moggies, for example, to be perennially stuck in the past, chewing over lost career opportunities, and tabbies to be forever getting ahead of themselves with their crippling excess of ambition?

Samson, the heavyweight marmalade cat who used to live across the road, had a bit of a Buddhist quality about him. Actually, the term that sprang to mind was more 'massive stoner' than 'Buddhist', but I had easily been able to imagine him at the meditation course I'd attended a couple of years ago, mindfully spreading loving kindness to his extended social circle or picturing his nostrils as caves and his breath as the wind blowing into them. I could not quite imagine Andrew – or Sven, as he was now called, two out of every five times Gemma and I referred to him – in the same scenario, but who knew what might happen, with a little persuasion and a calmer lifestyle?

I was convinced, by the noise that he made outside almost every night, that he wanted me to catch him and was just having trouble admitting it to himself. It was a throaty, rather feeble meow: one that seemed to snake and whisper through the gaps in my house's structure. To many people it might have been a meow that said 'I am a ghost cat, and I want to haunt you, but I am finding it a challenge, due to the fundamental problem that I am scared of my own tail.' To me it was a meow that said 'Please love me, feed me cooked meats, and make a warm, comfortable place next to your laptop for me to rest my head.' The moments when I caught him eating from the biscuit dispenser and he paused and stared at me became more prolonged and aching, allowing me to fall more in love with his defiant, yet somewhat vacant, moon face.

My other cats were often around at the time, and continued to mind their own business; only Shipley showed a degree of petulance about the situation. I was used to walking into various rooms of my house to be greeted by a group of cats giving me 'What do *you* want?' looks. But when one of them wasn't even mine, it became a bit galling. It was high time I rectified the situation, before Gemma and I properly considered the prospect of finding a home for another cat we'd never met – one who wasn't, to our knowledge, so desperate for food.

Gemma was now living with me in Norfolk around seventy per cent of the time, and living and working in Devon for the other thirty per cent. Andrew's timing was no coincidence. Surely he wanted to be the first cat we had co-owned, and he just needed that little bit of encouragement? Our plan was simple: the next time Gemma was here and we heard Andrew upstairs, we would creep up there. Gemma would bar the cat door, and I would leap on him.

There were, however, two large flaws in our thinking. First, there was Andrew's ability, while fairly loud in exiting the house, to enter it with enormous stealth. Due to these entrances I imagined him with tiny jewel thief's gloves on his paws, easing the catflap gently shut behind him with a grimace of pained concentration on his face.

Only if the house was utterly silent and our antennae were on full alert would we hear him arrive. This was a big ask in what was a loud and rather grouchy building. The mere clink into gear of my central heating often sounded like a goblin had done something unmentionable to a robot in the spare room and the robot had found the experience surprisingly enjoyable. How were you expected to listen out for an experienced cat burglar in that kind of environment? We were asking for almost impossibly tranquil circumstances: no Ralph meowing his own name, no Ralph snoring, no Shipley – now back to full fitness, with a personal volume control that once again went all the way up to eleven – telling people to piss off, no watching TV, no ducks outside having heated discussions about duck things.

Second, we lived in a house with two catflaps, the second having been installed on the top floor a few years earlier to give Ralph and Pablo more chance of entering and exiting the house without crossing claws. If Gemma and I blocked the top entrance, Andrew was swiftly down to the other one, and its 'in only' lock function was no match for a cat who had been surviving on his wits for more than year. Many, many co-ordinates had to be in place, and we weathered six weeks of near misses before, finally, the three of us found each other frozen in a stand-off in the kitchen, like hoodlums with raised guns in the closing scene of a Quentin Tarantino movie. I moved slowly towards Andrew and, as if in defeat, he accepted a gentle rub on the head. His fur had a rough quality to it, similar to Pablo's in the early days of his retirement from feral life. His ears were spotted with even more scabs and cuts than I'd expected, and he gave off a rather pungent odour. Upon inspection, his standard man parts were, as we suspected, very much intact. He didn't purr, but seemed to enjoy the contact, and made no attempt to run.

'Definitely a Sven,' said Gemma, joining in with the head rub.

We left Andrew-Sven in the small glassed-in room on the top floor of the house. The thinking behind this was that lots of windows would make him feel less like he was being incarcerated. The next morning, I was touched to find that he had moved from the chair where I'd left him into the wicker cat igloo so disdained by the other cats. This, I told myself, is what you get from a cat who's known hardship: a proper, non-complacent appreciation for items of furniture that have been built and purchased specifically with his or her comfort in mind. 'Andrew!' I called, and he woke up rather slowly, as if from a long deep sleep for which his body had been yearning for years.

Later that morning, in the vet's waiting room, Gemma and I continued to try out names.

'Gordon!' I called to Andrew.

'No way,' said Gemma. 'Not trustworthy enough. Bob!'

'No,' I said. 'I see Bob as more of a tabby name.'

'Colin! Rameses! Ethelbert! David! Wulfric! Don! Ken! Benjamin Netanyahu!'

'You're being ridiculous now. Actually, Ken's not bad.'

As Andrew-Sven-Ken sat on the vet's examining table, we continued.

'Roy! Pierce Brosnan!' cried Gemma.

'Grant! George!' I called.

'Yes!' replied George, the Californian vet, looking a little startled.

'Sorry! We were just trying out names for the cat.'

'Oh, I see,' George said, clearly relieved that I didn't want him to sit on my knee while I kneaded the skin at the back of his neck.

George broke the news that Andrew had severe ear mites, for which he would need a regular dose of treatment, as well as flea treatment and worming tablets, and a test for feline AIDS. Add this to the price of his neutering, and I was paying close on two hundred pounds that I didn't possess for the welfare of a strange cat whose future with me was by no means guaranteed.

Herein lies one of the reasons a vast number of cats are given away, particularly in the current economic climate. It's easy to picture cat ownership, unthinkingly, as a loose, inexpensive contract between you and a freelance employee: sure, you need to buy food, but everything else kind of takes care of itself, doesn't it? It's possible to be blinded by the seeming invincibility of kittens and forget that a cat's health is your responsibility too, and it requires its own monthly stipend, whether in the form of pet insurance or a fee allocated for future health mishaps. As a cat owner who is not made of money, at some point in the future it is likely that you will stand in a vet's surgery and ask yourself the question, 'Can I afford to pay

for this?' Then, if you're a decent person, you will ask
yourself the natural follow-on question, 'Can I afford *not*
to pay for this?' I knew what I was getting myself into
with Andrew when we captured him and took him to
the vet's: that there was every possibility that, after he'd
been through his cat MOT, he might escape or be bun-
dled off to live with my mum and dad, or with someone
else entirely. So – just as I had done a few months previously, when Shipley had been so ill – I told George to
give him the works.

'Have you thought that maybe Andrew is Chip?' I
asked Gemma, on the way home.

'You mean Sven? Noooo. Chip is very different. He's
much lankier, more spoilt. I'm beginning to think he's a
bit of a prat actually. Maybe we shouldn't adopt him after
all. He'll be OK. Everyone warms to Chip at first, until
they get to know him. He always lands on his feet.'

That evening, having brought him home again in his
new testicle-free state, we finally agreed on a name for
Andrew that we both liked: Graham. It was a moniker
that had all the trustworthiness of Ken but also brought
to mind the wearing of a quality wool cardigan. A Ken,
I felt, might have an intrepid side, a list of outdoorsy life
goals he'd want to tick off on his bucket list, but a
Graham would ultimately be happiest at home in front
of a fire. I didn't actually *have* a fire any more, as I'd paid
an angry builder a few years ago to knock down the wall

that my house's chimney was attached to, but we could cross that bridge when we came to it. The first thing was to see if Graham liked living here.

The following morning we received the good news that Graham was not FIV positive. This seemed to confirm that we'd finally found a fitting name for him. You sensed that a Graham would not be the kind of cat who slept around or abused drugs, and, if he did have occasional moments where he let his libido get the better of him, he would be careful to take the necessary precautions.

I took a few snaps of Graham with my cameraphone over the next couple of days and, if you overlook the one showing him freaking out and trying to find a secret passageway to freedom behind the coats hanging up near the front door, he appears quite content in all of them. On his first night, Shipley and Ralph had slunk casually into his room and each had an exploratory sniff of him, but they otherwise continued to appear indifferent to his presence, and he to theirs. The Bear had merely stared at him soulfully through the frosted glass of the doorway, like some grief-stricken black owl.

Andrew's escape, on the third night, was entirely down to my complacency and overeagerness for him to be 'ours'. We'd let him explore the rest of the house, and he'd not seemed to be in any rush to get anywhere else, so I'd suggested that we unblock the catflaps. Gemma thought this might be premature, but I reasoned that, if we didn't unblock them, we would be plunged back into a dark, archaic pre-catflap world of repeated door openings. When you have catflaps, it's all too easy to forget the miserable, minute-by-minute toil necessary in such a world. Nobody ever asked the question 'Who Let the Cats Out?' in a pop song because the answer is obvious: it was the same person who let them in again two minutes later, and out again two minutes after that. Doors are a classic example of that 'I hate this – it's fucking great!' mantra that seems to be part of the permanent internal monologue of all cats. Cats hate doors for the opportunities doors deny them to do exactly what they please, but they love them in equal measure, due to the opportunities they present to make humans their snivelling slaves. I knew, given the opportunity, that Ralph, Shipley and The Bear would be no different.

As it was, I had only moved the boxes and chairs with which I'd blocked the catflaps. I hadn't even progressed to stage two, the unlocking of the flaps themselves, and Graham was on the case. The second Gemma and I turned our backs, he was down to the bottom flap and had jemmied the lock, the mellow persona evident in the preceding forty-eight hours suddenly looking like a very clever act. Then he was out into the cool evening air, the catflap swinging on one hinge in his wake. A distant duck quacked on the lake beyond as if laughing at my foolishness.

I looked at Gemma. 'I think I've made a terrible mistake.'

'He'll be back,' she said.

'Raaaaaaaalph!' said Ralph.

In view of what he'd been through, it was probably quite surprising that Graham came back at all, let alone within a couple of days. If I had been homeless, and a kind stranger had taken pity on me, then put me in a glorified cage and taken me to a boxy building on a business park and had my testicles removed, I'd have made it my mission, after escaping, to put myself as far away from them as possible, and to return for ice-cold revenge, in the dead of night, long after the misdeed had slipped their mind. Instead, Graham simply made his returns more stealthy than ever, always arriving when we were in bed, shooting out the cat door the second he heard Gemma's footsteps or mine. Once again, the 'in-only' lock function proved no obstacle for his dextrous paws, and the one time I reached the catflap before he had chance to work the lock, he merely smashed it to pieces. Sitting next to it clad only in a pair of pyjama bottoms, I felt a new kind of forlornness: not just for the new catflap that would soon be added to Graham's ever-increasing bill, but because there was absolutely no way to explain what I'd done to him. I'm sure Shipley and Ralph had been feeling a little sore with me when they'd got home from neutering too, but I'd already built up a trust with them beforehand.

Sitting on that cold tiled floor, with another of Ralph's giant hairballs not six inches from my bare feet, I had one of those occasional moments of revelation, where you step outside yourself and realise just how far you've come from the person you once were. I thought of the thirteen-year-old me fantasising about playing on the right wing for Aston Villa; of the sixteen-year-old me convinced that his future would take place on the lush green fairways of the professional golf tour; of the twenty-something rock journalist me having a pepper-eating competition with the Foo Fighters or watching former Guns N' Roses guitarist Slash break off from an interview with him to stand on his hotel bed and play air guitar. Was this really what I had been reduced to as I approached my thirty-seventh birthday: a man sitting on a cold tiled floor at 1 a.m. in old, severely elastic-deficient pyjama bottoms, who, instead of buying the new clothes that he badly needed, paid for random, strange cats to have their balls removed?

One rare glimmer of hope occurred about three days later, when I looked out the window at dusk to see Ralph and Graham curled up on separate deckchairs down on the patio. I knew Graham would run away if I attempted to

catch him, so I left him there. Half an hour later, when I looked again, he was gone. As Gemma said, perhaps it was a sign that he just needed time, and would come back after all. That was, however, the last sighting for several days.

To add insult to injury, a text from Deborah arrived the following week. 'Want to come and meet our new cat?' she asked, attaching a picture of Graham.

'That's Graham!' I said, when she opened her front door to me half an hour later.

'Who's Graham?'

'I mean Andrew. Well, he's Graham now. We changed it after we caught him and got him neutered, but then he escaped again. It's a long story. Anyway, *why does he love you, and not us*? I mean, obviously, we had his balls cut off, but *apart* from that.'

'No, as I said, this isn't Andrew. I mean Graham. This one's very friendly. He's not around all the time and he's popped out again at the moment. I suppose it takes a bit of time for ferals to get adjusted. But he's coming in for food every day. Biscuit's very suspicious of him, but he and David get on like a house on fire. He's been all over him today, jumped on his lap and everything. We've decided to call him Alan.'

'But have you seen Graham close up?'

'No, but I've seen him around. He's different. Definitely a different cat.'

Back at home, I made a mental list of the facts:

1. Both cats were ginger.
2. Both cats had personas that had led their new

wannabe owners to give them names evoking men who might work as financial advisors.

3.   In exactly the same period when Graham had been getting to know Deborah and David, he had been absent from our house.

4.   Gemma and I had taken Graham to meet a man from California who had spoken in tender, reassuring tones to him, then drugged him and removed his bollocks.

5.   Deborah and David had not taken him to meet a man from California who had spoken in tender, reassuring tones to him then drugged him and removed his bollocks.

6.   The picture Deborah had shown me of Alan was actually of Graham.

It all seemed extremely suspicious, and over the following nights I would find myself lying awake, turning it over in my mind, much as a conspiracy theory fanatic might do with the specifics of the plane crashes in America on September 11th, 2001. With Shipley and Ralph's night-time rowdiness in full flow, I wasn't sleeping well anyway, and wondered if it might be time for me to take down the sign on the bedroom door that said 'CAT SERVICE STATION – OPEN 2am–5am', since it didn't seem to be working out for me.

'It's probably best if we just try not to think about him,' said Gemma, but it was easier said than done. On the evening before my birthday, it rained hard, and water thundered into the conservatory through the hole in the roof

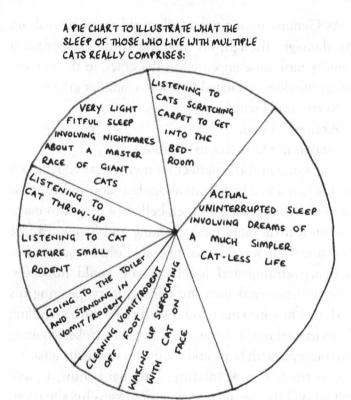

A PIE CHART TO ILLUSTRATE WHAT THE
SLEEP OF THOSE WHO LIVE WITH MULTIPLE
CATS REALLY COMPRISES:

VERY LIGHT FITFUL SLEEP INVOLVING NIGHTMARES ABOUT A MASTER RACE OF GIANT CATS

LISTENING TO CATS SCRATCHING CARPET TO GET INTO THE BED-ROOM

LISTENING TO CAT THROW-UP

LISTENING TO CAT TORTURE SMALL RODENT

GOING TO THE TOILET AND STANDING IN VOMIT/RODENT

CLEANING VOMIT/RODENT OFF FOOT

WAKING UP SUFFOCATING WITH CAT ON FACE

ACTUAL UNINTERRUPTED SLEEP INVOLVING DREAMS OF A MUCH SIMPLER CAT-LESS LIFE

made by Graham, which I'd thought I'd had mended. I couldn't help imagining him out there somewhere, soaked and shivering, wondering what that vaguely empty feeling towards the rear of his body was – that is, if Deborah was to be believed, and he wasn't curled up contentedly at this very moment in her and David's front room. I was being irrational. Since when had I seen a cat shiver just because of a bit of rain? But I had slipped into defeat mode again. I felt defeated by the house, defeated by cats.

As Gemma passed me another old towel to soak up the damage, though, an amazing thing happened: a friendly pink nose appeared in the crack in the conservatory window. Attached to it was a familiar ginger face.

'Sven!' said Gemma.

'Andrew!' I said.

'Graham!' the two of us chorused.

It was one of those perfect moments that you'd retell later, when asked by friends about how you and your cat came to live together, with embellished details to make it seem a little more heartwarming and lovely. Except this time there was no need to embellish, because it was as heartwarming and lovely as you could hope for. Graham sauntered into the conservatory, pushing his cold nose first into my hand then into Gemma's, sniffing about in a relaxed fashion, accepting our strokes, looking into our eyes with hope and – this was the really amazing part – trust. It was amazing, I thought, how a mere animal had the capacity to go away, assess his situation, and come back with a complete adjustment of attitude. He did smell a little more pungent than usual, but I thought it was the least we could do to invite him into the bedroom. He waltzed happily in, with Gemma trailing him.

'Hold on,' she said. 'He's got balls.'

I inspected the area in question. 'But ... how ... what ... That's impossible,' I said. 'They've grown back! They can't do that. Can they?'

As I looked in more detail at the cat in front of me, taking in his bulk and the patch of white on the top of his nose that was just a bit too big, I realised quite how blind I'd been. And then all the details I'd missed began to hit me, one after another, like objects falling out of a cupboard I'd hastily, carelessly filled weeks earlier. I had been alarmed at how big Graham had looked the other day, when he'd been sitting on the deckchair next to Ralph, but I hadn't really thought to question it.

I thought back to a night a couple of months earlier, not long after Shipley had been ill: another period where I'd not been getting much sleep, due to Graham's early-morning break-ins. Shipley had been making up for the valuable three or four days he'd lost, going on all sorts of mini-nocturnal adventures, and popping back after each one to tell me about it. I'd woken to the sound of cats fighting and worried it might be him, but, stumbling outside and up the stairs leading to the front of the house, I'd seen two ginger cats squaring up to one another, fur mohicans fully erect. I'd shooed them off with a sleepy, half-hearted 'Oi! Take it elsewhere!' and I'd identified one as Graham (or Andrew, as he was then known), but I'd been half asleep at the time, and summarily forgot about the incident. I had heard the noises of other cat fights in the night recently. But none in the last fortnight: the fortnight since Graham's balls had been removed.

This, then, must have been the battle that had played itself out for the last few months, beyond our awareness, in the pathways and nooks and undergrowth surrounding the Upside Down House: the story of two ginger cats, possibly even siblings, both of whom were looking for a home. There were two homes for them: homes owned by people who loved cats. Sadly, though, only one cat could ultimately stay in the locality. The smaller, less confident cat had been the original settler, and he'd fought bravely for his territory, but then he'd lost two vital things: small things, but things that made him feel like a man, that made him want to fight.

After that, it was all over. There could be only one victor, and we were looking at him.

'Hello, Alan,' I said.

'Hi, Alan,' said Gemma.

'*Meeooop*,' said The Bear, who'd come into the bedroom to see what all the fuss was about.

'Hi everyone,' said Alan, not with words, but with a powerful jet of urine, some of which sprayed the bedroom wall, but most of which landed on the curtains.

It seemed that Graham was lost for ever. A week became a fortnight, then a month. I looked for him outside every night, asked amongst neighbours, but there was no sign. I left food by the door, but it was snaffled by Alan, who – though never quite as friendly as he had been the night he'd pissed on the curtains – was now carrying on where Graham had left off, in terms of coming in through the catflaps and weeing on my Bill Withers records. I blamed myself, not Alan, for Graham's departure, but in a way it had been Graham's own decision: we had made it clear he had a home here, and if he'd really wanted it, perhaps he would have taken it. I'd been wrong to assume all ferals *want* a home. Some of them probably just want to eat.

'Of course, Chip's got his faults, but he would never have done any of this,' said Gemma, as we sat together on the floor, putting new protective polythene sleeves on the W–Z section of my albums for a second time.

I wondered what all this spelled for The Bear, who was often still seen by Deborah and David, staring in at Biscuit through the windows of their house. That candle he held for her may have flickered somewhat of late, but it was not about to go out just yet, and I couldn't imagine him feeling good that she now shared her house with a large, roughneck male cat from south Norfolk's mean lanes. I was glad that Alan had found a home with two cat lovers, though, and I enjoyed the comedy of hearing Deborah call 'Alllannn!' every evening. It brought to mind the pleasing mental picture of her and David adopting a small, rather naughty insurance clerk who ran free in their garden, buried his own faeces and batted for the local village cricket team at weekends.

Once again, I thought of those anonymous ferals and their gossip about me, picturing their reaction to all this, and the events that had led up to it.

'So Ginger Ron's called Alan now, and given up travelling to settle down? That's weird. Never saw that one coming.'

'Yeah, and the guy in the weird sixties house with the hole in the roof got Ginger Dave's balls cut off.'

'What? Man, that's harsh. I thought you said this guy

was a pushover. Ginger Dave could be a bit annoying, with that throaty meow of his, but he didn't deserve that.'

'I think it was done with good intentions, actually. It's like this guy's a charity, just for cat balls. I was thinking I might get mine done, actually. I'm tired of wanting to mount everything with a pulse. I feel like I'm chained to an idiot. I need some down time.'

'Are you serious?'

'I'm not the only one. Give up the sex life for an inexhaustible supply of free food – that's the way to go. Word's out on the lanes. I've got some of my old gang coming over from just outside Stowmarket next week. They've been living in this derelict farm, but it's being redeveloped and they're looking for a simpler existence. One that's not so dramatically governed by their hormones.'

'I can't believe this. You've changed, dude.'

We make a large proportion of the big decisions in our life in a weakened state. This is one of the reasons why, unless you're a person of extreme, calculated rationality, life rarely follows a straightforward pattern: big stuff more than often follows on directly from big stuff, like falling dominoes. A career change might come about as a reaction to a bad job experience. A relationship might well have more chance of getting off the ground because of the failed relationship that preceded it. A house will be bought in tribute to, or as a reaction to, a previous house.

Cat ownership is often similar. I was yet to make any very carefully planned decision regarding the adoption of a cat. The adoption of Ralph and Brewer had been inextricably linked to the chaotic excitement of a whirlwind marriage and a reckless move to a new county; the adoption of Shipley had been inextricably linked to the chaotic excitement of adopting Brewer and Ralph, combined with the chaotic excitement of seeing a nine-week-old Shipley jump over a small ornamental pond. Pablo and Bootsy had come into my life largely because of a failed mission to get a beagle and a rough calculation that its weight might compare to that of two small cats. Janet and The Bear had wandered into my life without any planning at all, leaving me no real choice in the matter. That's just the way it works, a lot of the time. But maybe I'm making excuses for Gemma and myself, hoping that the weakened state in which we found ourselves after the disappearance of Graham accounts, in some way, for the careless haste of our subsequent actions. Forgive us: the first thing we did, after realising he was not coming back, was to go straight out and get a kitten.

It was my birthday, after all.

Advice for New Kitten Owners

Procuring your kitten

All proper kittens grow on small furry trees. Some people purchase kittens from shops and supermarkets, to which the kittens are transported in cramped lorries, alongside other cute animals such as pygmy goats and puppies. Try to get your kitten straight from a furry tree if you possibly can, as it will be fresher and less likely to be bruised.

Make your kitten stand very still

When you get your kitten home, take it out of its basket, place it on a smooth, flat surface and ask it to stand very still and not make a noise. The kitten will be very disorientated in its new environment, so if it manages to heed your advice and not move for over twenty minutes, it's a good sign that the kitten has a stoical character and will be equipped to withstand life's setbacks with equanimity. After ninety minutes or so, tell the kitten it can relax, and reward it with a small snack: some muesli, perhaps, or three or four organically grown leeks.

Your kitten's first headache

Kittens are often plagued by headaches in the first three months of their lives, and can become irritable and monosyllabic as a result. Do not on any account try to treat one of your kitten's headaches with medication. Instead, make your kitten very comfortable in a darkened room, and sing softly to it. Try, maybe, one of the early love songs of David Gates and the band Bread, or 'Summer Breeze' by Seals and Crofts. If your singing is up to scratch, your kitten will be cured in less than an hour, and ready for its next adventure.

Don't waste time in getting your kitten started on literature

Don't make the mistake of delaying introducing your kitten to books, just because you know a good seven or eight months need to elapse before it is be able to read. Those it gravitates toward might seem inconsequential now but could serve as a useful early indicator of its future career, desires, temperament and worldview.

Kitten Baskets

In eighteenth-century England, Kitten Baskets were seen by rural folk as a surefire way to ward off evil. A Kitten Basket would traditionally contain various bits of loose material from the owner's old quilts and shirts, some herbs and a kitten, and would be presented to people moving to the village on the day of their arrival. The new residents would eat the herbs, keep the kitten in their front window overnight and return it to its owners in the morning, after which their house would be 'blessed' and delivered from future evil such as storm damage, plague, and randy wandering soldiers intent on taking the maidenheads of their daughters. The tradition of the Kitten Basket lives on in many counties, although not in Staffordshire, following the infamous Cannock Chase Kitten Basket Theft of 1864.

Slowly introduce your kitten to outdoor life
Introduce your kitten gradually to the outdoors. Before letting it go out on its own, ease your kitten into the outdoor life it will very soon be able to enjoy by showing it carefully, realistically illustrated pictures of the outside of your house. Try also placing the kitten behind a locked

window on a sunny day, standing on the other side of the window, waving to it, and pointing out exciting outdoor things such as trees, hammocks and wood pigeons.

Sleeping places your kitten will genuinely enjoy
It's a misconception that kittens like to sleep on blankets and jumpers. They actually much prefer to sleep in waste paper bins. Nobody is sure why this is, but some experts think it's related to the fact that waste paper bins often contain magazines, and kittens like to read before falling

asleep. Buy a waste paper bin that's slightly too big for your kitten, so it can grow into it. If there is no waste paper bin available, a kitten will generally compromise by sleeping on a toilet, or on the neck of a person aged between fifty-five and sixty-five.

Introducing your kitten to a cat who already lives with you
If you have an older cat, place it outside the house, then make it stare at the kitten through a window. This might seem cruel, but will actually make the old cat re-evaluate its life – something it's probably been putting off doing for far too long anyway – and face the future more realistically, acknowledging the limitations its age now imposes on it. This will ultimately help it to get on with the kitten on a more honest basis.

Kittens and their spirit world guardians

Unlike many ghosts, those of cats are very kind and well-meaning. It's entirely possible that, not long after you get your kitten, a cat ghost who happens to be haunting your area at the time will latch on to it and begin to whisper to it or hover mournfully over its waste paper bin at night. Don't be alarmed by this, and try not to shout or throw things at the cat ghost; it is probably very sensitive, especially if it is a new ghost and still self-conscious

about its non-corporeal state. More than likely the ghost is just trying to protect the kitten from dangerous things such as cars, dogs and the *Daily Mail's* Liz Jones. Soon, a beautiful friendship may even develop between the two of them, full of whispered secrets and perfect, tranquil moments, where they will watch the world go by whilst embracing tenderly.

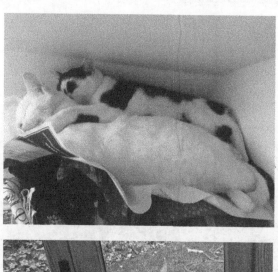

Testing your kitten for grip

A good early way to test your kitten's clinging power and agility is to throw your kitten extremely gently at a shed. If it sticks to the shed, that means it's a good kitten.

Your kitten's first dalliance with disco

The natural love of kittens for disco has been severely underdocumented over the years. Kittens like disco partly because of the freedom it gives them to express themselves, but also because, unlike Lindy Hop, salsa or other, trendier dance styles, it has very few 'rules'. A kitten can only dance to disco for up to twenty minutes at a time, so try not to be disturbed if it falls asleep in the middle of a disco move. This just means it is on 'boogie recharge'.

Try not to make your kitten's dinners too comfortable

At mealtimes, don't make things too easy for the kitten. Encourage it to stretch and work for its food. Ask yourself: Do I really want one of those 'nancy boy' overprivileged kittens who only eat weird, poncey cat foods with sweetcorn and croutons and crap in them, and are always banging on about how the world owes them a living? Do I really think my kitten wants to *be* one of those kittens? Remember: you'll be doing everyone a favour in the end.

Kittens and floristry

Many kittens enjoy floristry. In this area, the typical gender roles of the human world tend to be reversed. Very few female kittens like flower arranging, but for male kittens it is seen as a sign of masculinity and virility.

Set your kitten on the right musical path

Kittens are huge music fans, and are often much more likely to come and get their food to the sound of a popular rock hit than a whistle or the singsong call of their name. It's important to remember that while kittens often tell themselves they like credible but overrated bands such as The Clash or Radiohead, they are lying to themselves and in denial about their true love of 1970s progressive rock and acid folk. Once you've got your kitten settled, begin by playing it Pentangle's 1970 *Cruel Sister* LP or The Moody Blues' criminally

underrated *A Question Of Balance* from the same year, before moving on to the more bluesy, elongated and cosmic *Overdog* from a year later by The Keef Hartley Band. If the kitten makes a face like the one opposite, that means it approves.

Don't let your kitten eat a whole cow, a blanket, or a plug from the shower
Make sure your kitten doesn't eat any of these things. They are bad for it.

Don't allow your kitten to get too cocky

Once you've started to let your kitten run around outside, you'll notice it starting to get a little bit full of itself, thinking it's really shit hot for decking a twig, effeminately breaking a bee's wing or gleefully slapping about some of the more colourful, less invasive weeds in your garden. Try not to mock the kitten too blatantly for its efforts. Instead, subtly patronise it.

Try phrases like 'That's good – I'm sure a lot of other cats your age would feel that it was an achievement too, until they'd amassed more life experience', or 'I suppose it's all about perspective: that twig probably seems quite "Safari" if you've previously spent all your life in west London.' This will mean that the kitten will be easier to control and subjugate once it begins to meow properly, gets proper claws and starts wanting to use your bedroom as a cat service station in the middle of the night.

The Legend of Chimney Dog
Chimney Dog is a truly terrifying figure, stories of whose dark deeds have been passed down through kitten folklore for hundreds of years. A transsexual, soot-black hound with the back legs of a human blacksmith and the claws of a bitter and lonely former actress, he-she is said to climb down chimneys and steal kittens in the dead of night, when humans are asleep. Even if your kitten's elders have not told it about Chimney Dog, there will be

a deep, primal part of it that already somehow knows he-she is out there, waiting. If you find your kitten staring at your chimney with a fearful look on its face, more than likely it is thinking about Chimney Dog. Maybe best simply to block your chimney or get a wood burner or something?

Put big things around your kitten

By the time you've had your kitten a few weeks, your kitten will really be settling in, fully exploring your house and discovering its favourite plants to eat, places to sleep and objects from which to hang upside down. It

will be sneaking up on other cats and generally acting like a miniature version of Popeye Doyle in the early scenes of *The French Connection*. However, it's very important that you remind it at all times that it is, in fact, just a kitten. A good way of doing this is to place big objects near it or over it: feet and legs are good, as are bigger cats with shadowy portentous auras, inflatables, and oversized vegetables.

Your kitten and the self-employed workplace

As everyone knows, kittens aren't legally able to work until they are ten months old. In the meantime, however, they can be paid informally on a freelance basis for house and garden jobs, such as window cleaning, the planting of minor crops, and sweeping – although not the sweeping of chimneys, obviously, because of the whole Chimney Dog thing.

Encouraging your kitten to be self-aware
If your kitten misbehaves, don't shout at it. Instead, ask it to take a long hard look at itself: Is it the kitten it thinks it is? Has it been fooling itself, and glossing over the flaws in its personality?

Kittens who scrump

Not all kittens go scrumping, but there's every chance that, if your kitten lives in a rural area, it will get caught up in scrumping culture, due to peer pressure. If you find that your kitten has been scrumping, reprimand it, then take it to the house of the growers of the fruit that it scrumped and make it apologise to them. You might also want to revoke its disco privileges for a day or two, but don't be too harsh on it. Remember: scrumping is a relatively minor crime for adolescent kittens. Your kitten could be doing something much worse in this day and age: sniffing car exhaust pipes, say, or joining forces with the feral kittens to fight geese in the local park.

Send your kitten out to spend a night in a tree
The time-honoured 'Tree Night' is a harsh but necessary stage in a kitten's initiation. The big misconception about it is that it has to involve a big tree: an oak or giant redwood really isn't necessary. A moderate ash or fig, or even a slightly decrepit silver

birch, will suffice. The kitten might look fearful as it climbs towards the upper branches but, behind the veneer of pain, you will be able to see in its eyes that it knows you have its best interests at heart. As it reaches the pinnacle and finds a spot to rest for the next nine

hours, it will achieve a special kind of meditative calm and find itself truly living in the moment like never before. The following morning, you will be all the better off as the kitten greets you, shivering, at the top of your ladder and smothers you with kisses and compliments, and you will finally know that the difficult early stages are over, and you and your kitten are ready to properly start your new life together.

Oneupfurship

Something that Gemma and I found out about one another not long after we met was that we both had, in our fairly recent past, a tragic story involving a maverick black and white cat: a cat we'd fallen deeply in love with in the years immediately after we left our family homes then lost, very suddenly. Each of these cats had been the first we'd chosen for ourselves as adults, and each had been cruelly snatched away from us before they were fully grown.

Even now, barely a week went by where I didn't wonder what kind of cat Brewer, Ralph and Shipley's brother, would have grown into, had he not been run over in the summer of 2001. Ralph was a huge, hulking mouser, but just before his death, Brewer had already possessed around twenty per cent more body mass than his tabby brother. In terms of prey, he had worked his way up from mice to rabbits to pheasants, and was visibly mulling over the idea of his very first peacock scalp. I imagined of the still-thriving Brewer a parallel life as a comical beast: a cat of such formidable size that his tail entered a room a full thirty seconds after his head, but who was possessed of a preposterously babyish meow, which he deployed to lull the local wildlife – ducks, herons, dogs, a particularly large and proud horse down the road who resembled the 1970s rock star Todd Rundgren – into a false sense of security.

Rod was much more of a softy. He'd been tiny in 2007 when Gemma had adopted him, and was still smaller than ninety-five per cent of male cats seventeen months later, when he was hit by a car outside her flat in Plymouth. He'd never really liked to go out very much, and preferred the company of people to other cats. 'I know some cats like baths, but he *really* liked baths,' Gemma told me. 'He'd try to jump in every time I was in one. He was a maniac. He loved sleeping in the fruit bowl, and climbing up onto the door frame and leaping off it. He'd do it with his legs splayed in this weird way, nothing like a cat at all. He also trusted everyone, which used to worry me.'

In many ways, the photo we received at the end of May 2012 was much like hundreds of others of absurdly sweet black and white kittens needing adoption that I'd been sent by readers of my first two books about my cats. The difference was the black and white cat history Gemma and I shared, the cooling of her ardour for the apocryphal Chip, and the fresh, gaping space in our lives that Graham had formerly occupied. That, and the fact that Roscoe, with her Batman mask face, white tuxedo, and a tail that appeared to have had its tip dipped in white paint, was an almost cartoon-perfect example of what we'd started to imagine as our next cat: a good solid version of what most people probably immediately think of when their mind focuses on the phrase 'classic cat'. The kind of kitten that, when it was older, you might see staring back at you from the window of a pretty, wisteria-clad cottage as you strolled down a country lane in summer, in a way that said 'Yep, I'm a cat. What do you plan on doing about it?'

That was what we called her: Roscoe. We decided on the name with remarkable ease, considering our recent track record. It was a nod to several things: the magical song of the same name by the folksy, American Civil War-obsessed rock band Midlake, which we'd listened to on our way to collect her; our recognition of some early tomboyish hints about her character; and my thinking that I'd had a couple of boy cats with girl names in the past and it was time to even the score. There was also our belief that, if you called a kitten Roscoe, it could hardly be anything else but great. We were, however, quickly disabused of this notion.

It might have happened at a moment of weakness, but over time I have come to remember our adoption of Roscoe as a demonstration of remarkable restraint on my part. When I adopted Shipley, Ralph and Brewer, I walked into a stranger's house planning to come away with two cats, at the most, and ended up with three. When I adopted Bootsy and Pablo, all I'd initially been in the market for was a beagle. Jazzmine, who'd sent me the message about Roscoe, had not one but three kittens that she wanted to give away, all of which lived with her in her house in west London.

I knew her ultimate hope was that all of them would stay together, and that however strongly Gemma and I had resolved only to take one, we would waver once we saw the three of them sleeping in a tiny bundle, or running up the back of a sofa. As it turned out, it was an even greater test of our powers of resistance than we'd imagined: not only had I forgotten what an onslaught of cute a roomful of three kittens can be, there was something very familiar about Roscoe's brother and sister. Roscoe was every bit as loopy, spirited and friendly as Jazzmine had promised and, within minutes of her introduction to Gemma and me, was climbing cheerfully along our shoulders. Her equally energetic black and white brother, however, was an almost exact hybrid of Rod and Brewer; while Gemma and I didn't say so out loud, we both noticed it immediately and told each other so with our eyes.

Her sister, meanwhile, was familiar in an even more unexpected way. I'd never had the bittersweet privilege of knowing The Bear in his angst-ridden kittenhood, but I'd seen the sole photo of his kitten self that Dee had possessed when I met her, and it bore an uncanny resemblance to the four-month-old kitten I was looking at now. All of Roscoe's family's eyes were big and button-like, but those of this black cat seemed to carry an extra knowledge and wariness. 'This one is easily the most intelligent of the bunch,' Jazzmine confirmed. The Bear had tried his best with other cats all his life, but he couldn't get away from the fundamental fact that they were intellectually beneath him. Had I finally found the cat – a female cat, no less – with whom he could have the cultural and political debates he'd long hankered for? The image of the two of them sitting on The Bear's favourite bookshelf, like a pair of all-knowing black owls, was almost irresistible.

Somehow, we stayed strong. Driving back up the M11 towards Norfolk from Jazzmine's house with Roscoe alone in the basket on the back seat of the car, we were feeling pretty pleased with ourselves – smug, even – as if we were a couple of hardcore smokers who'd unexpectedly found a couple of quality menthol cigarettes in a pocket and each said, 'No, *actually*, I won't.'

It wasn't until we arrived home that everything started to go wrong. Now I think about it, though, the switch probably took place at Birchanger Green services, just outside Bishop's Stortford. Gemma and I had taken turns to go inside and use the toilet, so one of us was always with Roscoe, but while I'd been in the car I'd become distracted by an email on my phone from an editor. As I attended to it, the catnappers must have very gently eased open the rear door, unclicked the cat basket's lock, and made the swap.

I have to give them credit: they'd done their research. The she-devil kitten they replaced Roscoe with was an almost perfect match. Same white socks, tuxedo, Batman-mask face and button eyes. Same white-tipped candle tail. This tiny, furious monster slept peacefully as we progressed through Essex and Suffolk, but once at its new home, it began a campaign of terrible destruction, slinking out of its basket to hiss and growl at everything in its wake.

Admittedly, we did some pretty thoughtless stuff to Roscoe – or her doppelgänger, if that's what this kitten really was – in those first seventy-two hours with her. There was the moment when I stood on the opposite side of the kitchen to her and sliced a bagel in half directly in her eyeline, or when Gemma loudly sneezed a mere seven feet from her face, or – perhaps most unforgivably of all – the time on the second afternoon when I said, in a soft, encouraging voice, 'Would you like some of these overpriced turkey chunks, perhaps – maybe they would calm you down?' Looking back, I am thankful that we had the kindness not to do anything really hurtful, such as vacuum, or play the album by 1970s progressive rock band Spooky Tooth that I'd recently purchased, as I fear we might not be here to tell the tale.

The noises emerging from Roscoe's mouth were something I'd never expected to hear from any less than a medium-sized animal. Actually, that's untrue. Some of them might not have been all that surprising if, say, they'd emerged from an iguana that had received some particularly bad news about its family, or maybe a raven that was having a lot of trouble shaking off a chest infection. From a kitten, however, they were unexpected. They only grew worse when we attempted to make a gesture to get her more comfortable with her environment, such as showing her the stairs ('KAKkkkkkkcchssssssss!') or introducing her to a catnip mouse (Awaaaaggheeeh!').

'How is everything?' texted Jazzmine, not long after we woke up on Roscoe's second morning in the house. 'Is she settling in OK?'

'I'm afraid not,' I replied. 'Not sure if you spotted this yourself, but as it turns out, she is actually the miniature progeny of the monster who destroyed New York in the film *Cloverfield*. We've all tried to make it work as best we could, but after a long discussion, most of which involved her sitting behind a spider plant and going "Keeecheagggggggggh" at us, we've opted for an amicable separation. I've pointed her back in your direction. I'm hoping National Express is OK with you? Her coach gets into Victoria Station at fourteen minutes past ten. She'll be the one sitting on her own, the one who all the other passengers are cowering from in abject terror.' I didn't really write any of that, but it would have been a more frank assessment of the situation than my actual reply: 'Not bad. She's a little subdued, but I'm sure she'll be OK.'

That afternoon, I decided to be a bit more honest with Jazzmine. 'Has Roscoe always been OK with other cats?' I asked.

'Oh yes, very much so,' replied Jazzmine. 'She was born in a house full of cats, so she's always been ever so sociable. I hoped your cats would accept her, as I know she'll like them. Why do you ask?'

'Oh, nothing too much to worry about,' I replied. 'I'm just slightly concerned that she would like to slowly torture them then eat all of their kidneys. I'm sure they'll all start getting on soon.'

In truth, it seemed that Roscoe's rage was too absurdly tiny and ineffectual to bother my cats. As she hissed and practised her bonsai growl at Ralph and Shipley, they appraised her in the manner a busy office worker might appraise a small, ugly insect he'd spotted moving around on top of a pile of loose papers he'd left next to his desk for a secretary to shred. The Bear came over and had a couple of analytical sniffs, which received a feisty rebuke, but didn't have a lot to say on the matter, save for aiming a look in my direction that eloquently conveyed his despair at my continued habit of needlessly complicating my own life.

Gemma took a photo of me holding Roscoe at around this point, and we both went on to think of it as the one that encapsulated her first few days with us. Roscoe's tiny mouth, wide open, articulates her fury at all the recent woes that have befallen her. I look a bit baggy-eyed, but I'm grinning, in the manner of a man who has just found out that dragons, while no less angry than the tales written about them suggest, have lovely soft fur and are actually only one-thousandth of their reported size. Beneath that grin, however, is a well-hidden layer of worry. 'What if I've just been lucky?' I'm asking myself. 'What if I've just had a series of unusually lovely cats, and I'm about to be plunged into the harsh, bilious, affectionless reality of cat adoption that most people go through with man's best frienemies?'

Every so often during those first three days, Gemma and I gently encouraged Roscoe to sleep on one of the many soft surfaces we'd provided for her, but she preferred to sit sourly on floors and sideboards, as if in stubborn protest at this austere and forsaken eastern land that she'd been dragged to from the cosmopolitan comfort of west London. We gently encouraged her to use her litter tray, but it remained, to all appearances, untouched. A cuddle, meanwhile, was entirely out of the question.

I began to look upon Ralph, Shipley and The Bear with fresh eyes. Could I really say these cats had ever caused me any trouble? None of them had ever seriously injured me or one of my house guests, or given me cause for concern with his debauched, irresponsible lifestyle. For many years, each of them had kept their faeces and what they did with it mercifully far away from me, in the open air. They even each said a happy good morning to Gemma and me every day: Ralph with a chirrup, The Bear with one of his happier *meeeoops*, and Shipley with a noise that, while it translated to something like 'How are you doing, douchebag?' always seemed to have a fundamentally affectionate undertone to it. And now what had I done? I'd gone out, and, in my thoughtless greed, got a younger model. I may as well have written them a note explaining that their love was no longer enough for me. If Roscoe truly was a monster, I deserved every bit of hardship she was going to put me through.

By her fourth night with us, I – who'd spent, if you overlooked a short period in my early twenties, getting on for four decades living with cats – was losing hope, and Gemma – she from the hardcore dog-loving family, whose conversion to cat servitude had only taken place during the last few years – was playing the role of optimist. 'Maybe we should have taken her brother or her sister as well?' I said, as Roscoe scowled out at the two of us from behind a piece of 1960s West German pottery, as if making a cutting comment with her eyes about not just my presence, but my taste too.

'I think she just needs time,' said Gemma.

I was baffled: I'd heard about problem kittens who'd had rough starts in life, but in Roscoe's short past there was obviously nothing but kindness. Jazzmine had made it clear to us that if everything didn't work out with Roscoe, she still had a very loving home back in London, but I'd had the heartbreaking experience of 'returning a cat' once before – a black almost-panther called Raffles who in 2005 had made it his mission to drive Ralph, Shipley, Janet and The Bear out of the house, preferably to a different continent – and I'd sworn to myself that I would never do it again. I knew Roscoe could not keep up this level of icy resentment for ever – it would be too exhausting for her – but I saw a difficult decision on the horizon, even if it thawed into a mere cool disdain and fury. Perhaps I could cope: one sociopath cat out of four wasn't a bad ratio, was it?

I was trying to be realistic, but in doing so, I was projecting myself too far into the future, taking my eye off the present, and, while I did so, the present nipped in and surprised me. That night, in the early hours, as Gemma and I slept, the catnappers who'd snatched the original Roscoe at the service station a few days earlier broke quietly into the house and switched the two cats back. I'll never know what made them do it, but it was a reassuring demonstration that even bad people can sometimes have a conscience. I'm not sure where they'd been keeping the original Roscoe for the previous three days, but I assume it wasn't anywhere too traumatic, as she seemed pretty carefree when she greeted me the next morning, arriving in the kitchen with her paws in the air. I reached out for one and touched it, and she let out a small, friendly quasi-meow.

It was a flabbergasting, beautiful high five to go alongside the eclectic morning hellos of Ralph, Shipley and The Bear. When I picked her up, I wouldn't say she was exactly ecstatic, but there was none of the rigid anger I'd felt before. I took her into the bedroom, placed her on the bed beside Gemma, who'd just emerged from the shower, and the two of us watched, stunned, as the perfect kitten – the same perfect kitten we'd met at Jazzmine's house – executed a series of small somersaults, around and over our bodies.

It was not until we returned upstairs that we found the true explanation for Roscoe's transformation. Over the last few days, the litter we had put out for her had remained virtually unchanged in shape and texture, save for a couple of small wet patches. I'd heard a loud scraping sound the previous afternoon and had rushed upstairs, hoping for the best, but found The Bear in the litter: not, from what I could gather, putting it to its intended use, but happily splashing about in it like a granddad who'd reached some kind of cathartic end point in a stressful period in his life and decided to relive his childhood in a neighbour's paddling pool.

There was always the possibility that something of Roscoe's lay under there, or – though I didn't want to face up to the possibility – had been deposited in one of the nooks in the house where she'd been hiding out. But we hadn't seen her in the litter tray, and we worried how almost four days without a bowel movement might have been affecting her. Clearly, it had been affecting her more than we could have imagined, as in the tray now was the single biggest kitten turd either of us had ever clapped eyes on. A turd so huge, it could probably have beaten one of Ralph's most formidable hairballs in a fight. A turd that contained within its dark textures all the fury of the last few days.

'I think it could be alive,' said Gemma.

'It's bigger than her head,' I said. 'Actually, no. It's bigger than two of her heads.'

'OK,' said Gemma. 'Here's how we work this. You deal with that. I'll make a cup of tea.'

Lots of people experience irregular bowel movements in a new place. I used to have a friend – who for purposes of tact, I'm going to call Benedict, since I've never had any friends called Benedict, and am fairly unlikely to do so – who once admitted to me that he found it impossible to move his bowels for the first three or four days of any period he spent away from home. Benedict had tried everything from a fibre-heavy diet to meditation, to no avail. He just had to wait the constipation out, until his body adjusted to its new surroundings, and he knew after that it would be OK. Maybe that was what had happened to Roscoe too? She'd frozen up at first, but finally something inside her had decided it was OK – that there was nothing to fear in this place after all – and now the holiday could properly start.

I had made the decision to wait for a little while to tell my parents about Roscoe. During my mum's last visit, Shipley had perpetrated one of his most sneaky and vicious attacks on The Bear to coincide with our evening meal, and since then she'd been making more noises about helping me out by separating the two of them. I knew she felt I already had too many cats, and I could anticipate her faintly despairing disapproval at the idea of one more. My parents are born worriers, and the way I saw it, I wasn't lying by not telling them about Roscoe; I was just editing the truth for their own good. My plan was to wait until Roscoe was completely settled in and had become so irresistibly, infectiously happy it would be impossible to disapprove of her presence in any way. Then I would break the news. Obviously, my last, similar plan involving delaying the introduction of a cat to my parents hadn't worked out too well, but this one was falling into place quite nicely. Roscoe was still a little unsure about being picked up, but in the fortnight since The Day of the Enormous Turd, she was nothing but delightful. There was still a vague feeling that she was a blank canvas, but her foibles and quirks were slowly starting to reveal themselves. My top ten of these fluctuated from day to day, but at this point could probably be listed, in no particular order, as:

1. Sitting on the side of the bath and meowing at the water in it, as if pained by its beauty.
2. Watching televised sport with rapt attention.
3. Licking my armpit.
4. Getting all up in Shipley's grill and giving him a taste of his own medicine.
5. Running up the side of the shed.
6. Walking on hind legs and doing 'wavy paws' prior to food time.
7. Trying to beat the crap out of the evil kitten in the 'small window' (mirror) in the bedroom.
8. Going absolutely nuts and rolling all over Gemma and me at any point that we had a towel wrapped around us.
9. Doing a vertical take-off in an attempt to get quickly from one side of the bed to the foot moving tantalisingly about under the duvet on the other.
10. Going up to a dead vole killed by Shipley and growling at it, then pawing it three inches to the left, as if in the belief that that officially meant she could take the credit for catching it.

The following week, I put many of these facts, and a few others, in a convenient email digest to my mum,

along with three of the sweetest photos Gemma and I
had taken of Roscoe: one showed her stretched out happily inside a padded Jiffy bag, in another she was
sneaking up on The Bear from behind as he did a 'you
just can't get the convincing stalkers these days' face,
and in the third she sat companionably with one of my
old trainers, as if believing it to be a new, trustworthy
friend.

I felt pretty pleased with my public relations skills, but, when a reply popped into my inbox half an hour later, I braced myself for a small telling-off: something at least along the lines of the times when my mum saw the amount of empty crisp packets in my car or the state of my garden shed. Instead, what I saw was a picture of a tiny black and white kitten.

The kitten shared a colour scheme with Roscoe, but that, and the fact that they were both clearly of feline descent, were all the two of them had in common. This kitten was far more white than black, smaller than Roscoe, and – though this might have been partly to do with the position in which it was curled up – its head appeared to be roughly the same size as its torso. Around its mouth and on its nose were splotches of black, as if someone had used it as a furry Rorschach test. I felt that my mum was sending me some kind of coded message, but I had no idea what. Was she using this kitten's faintly beleaguered face as an abstract form of semaphore to demonstrate her own disapproval at my kitten? Was she suggesting I should have adopted this kitten instead of Roscoe? Or maybe she hadn't seen the text of my email, had misunderstood, and thought I was challenging her to a game of Who Can Send a Photo of the Sweetest Black And White Kitten?

'What is *that*?' I asked her on the phone a few minutes later.

'That's Pusskin. That's what I'm calling him for now. He's our new kitten.'

'Where's he from?'

'Next door. Casper's house, although he's not related. I'm a bit unsure about him at the moment. He doesn't seem to have much of a personality. I still prefer Casper. Next door's other cat had a litter recently, and they said a few were going spare, so we thought we'd give him a go. Your dad's still a bit uncertain too.'

'What about Casper?'

'I suppose he's just going to have to deal with it. The fact that he already knows him will probably help.'

'So you decided to get a kitten, and I got a kitten. At exactly the same time.' (This was a white lie, in order to stay consistent with my email, in which I'd told my mum that Roscoe had arrived only last week.)

'Yes. It is a bit weird, isn't it? I would say I think you're silly for getting another, but I suppose I don't have a leg to stand on. She looks very nice.'

I had hypothesised many different reactions to Roscoe from my mum: utter disbelief, frowning exasperation, resigned acceptance ... that special voice she does when she says 'Oh, *Tom*', leading me to believe I've not only let her down, but myself down, too. What I hadn't expected was a kitten-based retaliation.

That first picture began a pattern that would last for the next couple of months: a kind of kitten one-upmanship played out in the form of photos and progress reports. There was no reluctant, Roscoe-style teething period for my mum and dad's kitten. From about two hours into his first day in their house, he became a force of nature: a tiny fur whirlwind who, if he was awake, was either smashing something (an expensive sculpture of a bird and a vase my dad had bought my mum many years ago for their tenth wedding anniversary were early casualties), purring at something or stealing something. They named him Floyd, after the late TV chef Keith, whose lust for life he appeared to share. The name was my dad's choice, and one that wasn't so much embraced as accepted by my mum, who had vetoed my dad's earlier suggestions of naming him 'FLOB', after the cousin who'd led my dad's teenage gang in the 1960s, or 'DIRTY BERTIE', and mine of Rory, as a shortened version of Rorschach. I'm not sure if my mum was putting on the nonchalance a bit during her first conversation about Floyd, but, whatever the case, it lasted about five minutes. From then on, she was smitten in a way that was impossible to hide.

'Have you ever tried throwing a ping-pong ball for yours?' she said. 'Floyd loves it. You must try it.'

I thought of the three ping-pong balls that were permanently scattered around my living room, one of which had been the focal point in a game of football between Ralph and me the last time my mum had been to my house. 'No,' I said. 'You're right. I must try that some time.'

'So what should I buy him?' she asked me a few days later from her mobile phone, whilst in her local pet shop. 'He needs a scratch post. There's one here that seems to have a slide on it. Should I get that one? Will he use the slide? This morning Floyd ran straight into the bedroom and gave me a kiss. Do yours ever do that?'

It was as if my mum had forgotten that I had learned almost everything I knew about living with cats from the two decades I had spent living with her, my dad and their assortment of felines. It had been almost five years since Daisy's death, but now all the joy, frustration and comedy of cat ownership was coming back to my mum, bit by bit. It confirmed what I had believed all along: that she'd spent the last few years in denial about her status as a natural cat owner.

More surprising was my dad's instant bonding with Floyd, which, I found out, included carrying him around in the pocket of his fleece, and taking afternoon naps together. 'I'VE SOLVED THE MYSTERY OF WHY WE HAVE UNDERARM HAIR,' he told me. 'IT'S SO KIT-TENS CAN NEST IN OUR ARMPITS.'

Having seen that initial photo of Floyd, looking so delicate and tiny, I had worried about how he might deal with the phenomenal racket that would be an immutable feature of his daily life chez my dad. Daisy had been a mixed-up cat with the unusual trait of purring when she was angry and hissing during rare moments of content-ment. She'd never really let anyone get close to her, and her list of fears had been long and intricate, including everything from Yorkshire terriers to colanders, but her real nemesis was my dad. Upon hearing his booming voice and heavy footfall, she had made herself scarce behind sofas and under beds, later retaliating during the periods when he was working at his desk by breaking his concentration with a series of high-pitched, neurotic meows. More and more, as Daisy got old, I sensed that the meaning of her yowling was less 'Give me food!' and more 'I don't belong in this frightening world, and feel fearful and confused, especially by this man who is constantly bellowing enthusiastically about African pop music and his dislike for *Grand Designs* presenter Kevin McCloud!' But my dad's permanently cranked-up volume control did not bother Floyd in the slightest. He was a cat without hang-ups: confident, inquisitive, sociable, boisterous – all qualities that my dad admired.

'LOOK AT THIS,' my dad said, barely a minute after Gemma and I arrived at my parents' house on our maiden Floyd visit. He pointed to an Action Man figure suspended from the ceiling over the staircase by a piece of elastic, with a toy mouse wedged between its legs. My dad pulled on the elastic and, seemingly out of nowhere, a tiny kitten – though significantly bigger than he'd looked in the last photograph I'd seen of him, only a week ago – sprang into the air, and wrestled Action Man to the ground. I thought for a moment about asking why, at the age of sixty-two, my dad owned an Action Man, but the answer seemed potentially too long-winded, especially following a three-hour drive, so I decided to leave it. 'I MADE THAT FOR HIM,' he said. 'HE LOVES IT.' He led us into the living room, where, by my first count, at least 787 different cat toys, ranging from the high end to the truly makeshift, were strewn. 'STAY THERE. I'VE GOT SOME TEETH TO SHOW YOU THAT I FOUND BURIED IN THE GARDEN. I'VE BEEN UP SINCE FIVE.'

Over the next couple of days, we watched as Floyd wolfed down the expensive tuna my mum and dad had bought for him, chased ping-pong balls and climbed up our legs, my dad never far from him at any time, watching him with the same kind of pride with which a boxing promoter might watch the new protégé who has reignited his career. Floyd wasn't old enough to go out in the garden yet, but a few days ago my mum had found my dad out there with Floyd in his fleece pocket, conducting a personal guided tour. 'THERE'S AN AMAZING WASPS' NEST IN THIS SHED,' she'd overheard him telling their kitten. 'YOU'LL PROBABLY WANT TO AVOID THAT. AND THIS IS COMPOST CORNER. I SOMETIMES SLEEP HERE.'

I didn't know what it felt like to have a brother and, while I'd come close to finding out what it might be like in my encounters with a VW Golf my dad had owned a few years ago and been especially fond of, I was now getting a true insight. It wasn't even as if my dad restricted himself to the fun aspects of raising Floyd. 'I'VE STARTED LINING HIS LITTER TRAY WITH PHOTOS OF JEREMY CLARKSON,' he explained. 'IT'S REALLY SATISFYING. IT'S A SHAME YOU DON'T GET VEGETARIAN CATS, THEN I COULD COMPOST EVERYTHING AFTERWARDS. HAVE YOU NOTICED THAT EVERYONE WHO'S GOING TO BE IN THE OLYMPICS THIS YEAR IS CALLED BEN OR PIPPA?'

Upon her first couple of encounters with my dad, Gemma had reacted much more nonchalantly than some of my previous girlfriends. Now, though, she was getting the full treatment – not least the following day when the four of us left Floyd at home for the afternoon and went for a walk on the Nottinghamshire–Derbyshire border, taking in the limestone gorge at Creswell Crags, with its recently discovered Paleolithic caves. 'TOM'S MUM TOOK A PHOTO OF ME ON THE FLOOR, PRETENDING TO WRESTLE THAT LAST YEAR,' my dad explained to my girlfriend, pointing at the hyena in the visitor centre.

In some ways, this was how I'd envisaged my next relationship all along: a few good months, then the moment when my new partner realised exactly what she was getting herself into, genetically speaking, and backed out. I accepted that, and if she called it quits now, I couldn't complain. But, amazingly, Gemma seemed to be holding tough. As my dad scraped a line behind him in the sandy path with a stick he'd found, to illustrate just what a tiny portion of the planet's history had involved humans, she seemed to be genuinely interested. That, as he explained this, my dad was wearing a comedy Salvador Dali moustache he'd purchased from the Welbeck Abbey visitor shop was further testament to her patience and listening skills.

On the way back to the car, I nipped into the undergrowth, picked a nettle and ate it. I did this partly because nettle-eating – which, to be done successfully, requires the neutralisation of the nettle's sting by folding its leaves inwards, then placing them between your molars – was a skill I'd learned not long ago on a weekend foraging trip Gemma and I had taken to the Brecon Beacons, but also because I wanted to prove to my dad that the notion of free will existed.

His timeline in the dust had led him on to one of his main topics: predestination. Specifically, his belief – from an atheistic perspective – that all choice is an illusion.

'I CAN'T BELIEVE YOU JUST DID THAT,' he said. 'EUGH. YOUR MOUTH IS GOING TO SWELL UP AND YOU'RE NOT GOING TO BE ABLE TO EAT EVER AGAIN. AND I SAW A DOG DO A WAZ THERE EARLIER.'

'Maybe so, but that's beside the point,' I said. 'A moment ago, I hadn't even thought about eating the nettle, then, very suddenly, I decided I would. In a split second, I changed the course of history: not only mine but the history of everyone who comes into contact with me. Nothing can ever be the same again. Also, you're wrong. It tastes lovely, actually.' I felt that, if I were to let on that I had got the folding of the nettle wrong, and that the inside of my cheek was now throbbing slightly, it might somehow undermine the strength of my philosophical argument.

'THAT PROVES NOTHING,' said my dad. His false moustache wobbled precariously as he spoke. 'YOU JUST THINK YOU CHOSE TO EAT THE NETTLE. HOW CAN YOU BE SURE IT WASN'T ALWAYS GOING TO HAPPEN?'

I looked across at Gemma. She still seemed surprisingly unfazed.

'I just know.'

'YOU DON'T. ALL THIS WAS ALWAYS GOING TO HAPPEN. ME DRAWING THAT LINE IN THE

DIRT, YOU EATING THAT NETTLE WITH THE DOG PISS ON IT. ALL PREDETERMINED.'

Using some more of my free will, I chose to let the subject go. It's hard to have a serious debate with a man wearing a plastic Salvador Dali moustache, and I knew that when my dad was discussing predestination, there was little you could do to make him see sense. On holiday in 1984, he had wound his friend Malcolm up so much by discussing predestination that Malcolm pushed him off a small cliff in France. Discussing predestination was one of the main signs my dad was enjoying a country walk, along with rhapsodising about bulls and retelling stories about the O'Dohertys, an abundant neighbouring family on the council estate where he grew up. For all his excitability, though, he seemed a little more anxious than usual on the last stretch of today's walk, and was keen to get back to check on Floyd.

'KEEP IN!' he told my mum, Gemma and me as we walked along the grass verge back to the car. 'I'D LOVE TO GO TO ZAIRE. LOOK AT THE SIZE OF THOSE STABLES. WE NEED TO HURRY UP A BIT NOW. THE O'DOHERTYS ALWAYS HAD ANIMALS IN THEIR HOUSE. ONCE I LIFTED UP THEIR SOFA AND THERE WERE ABOUT TWENTY PINK MICE UNDERNEATH IT.'

When we arrived back at my parents' house, Floyd bounded up to my dad, who collected him in his arms. 'HOW ARE YOU DOING, OUR KID?' he asked. 'DID YOU MISS ME?' Floyd replied in the affirmative with the kind of purr from which you could probably power entire

music festivals. It was a comical noise in exactly the
opposite way to Brewer's crying baby meow, which had
become comical towards the end of his life: a huge sound
transposed to the body of a miniature cat. A few minutes
later, my mum discovered that, while we'd been out,
Floyd had done a wee in one of her aspidistras. She
seemed a little annoyed, but my dad responded very
calmly. 'IT'S OK,' he said. 'I'M GOING TO MAKE HIM
WATCH *WHITE FANG, THE COURAGE OF LASSIE*
AND *BEST IN SHOW* LATER AS PUNISHMENT.'

On various occasions in the last couple of days, my
dad had claimed that Floyd was 'THE BEST CAT
EVER'. As someone who lived with The Bear, I took
issue with this, but I supposed it was a matter of personal taste. Some were drawn towards displays of
physical showboating, when it came to cats, while others
preferred subtle intellectual stimulation. I had to admit
I'd fallen pretty hard for Floyd. He was an irrepressible
presence, a cat seemingly without neuroses – constantly
alert, but in an 'explorer' way, not an 'is something about
to attack me?' way. That evening, he took turns on each
of our laps, but ultimately settled on my dad, who held
forth on his recently rediscovered love of whisky
('WHEN I'M NINETY-FIVE I'M GOING TO TAKE
GLENFIDDICH INTRAVENOUSLY AND WATCH
DAD'S ARMY EPISODES BACK TO BACK'), the
amphibians in his garden pond ('NEXT SPRING I'M
GOING TO PUT A TOY FROG IN THERE FOR THE
LONELY UGLIER FROGS TO MATE WITH; LAST
YEAR THEY HAD TO MAKE DO WITH AN

APPLE'), the times that he used to bully my uncle Paul by playing him experimental jazz records by Sun Ra and Ornette Coleman ('I THINK HE WAS MORE OF A ROD STEWART MAN BUT HE WAS TOO POLITE TO SAY SO') and his new-found appreciation of the feline ('ONE OF THE GOOD THINGS ABOUT CATS IS THAT, UNLIKE DOGS, THEY DON'T COME UP TO YOU IN THE STREET AND TRY TO HAVE SEX WITH YOUR LEG!'). After half an hour of this, the two of them fell into a deep sleep – Floyd in an unusual pose, with one paw stretched into the air, that brought to mind the phrase 'death by disco'.

I wondered what it was about Floyd that had captured my dad's heart where many other cats and kittens hadn't. Was it his doglike ability to play 'fetch' with his toy mouse? Those Rorschach splotches on his nose and the way they somehow made his facial expression appear even more constantly intrepid than it already was? His baritone purr? 'I was wondering that too,' said my mum. 'And then I realised what it was. Have you noticed something? Floyd is always either completely switched on, or completely switched off. Who else do we know who's like that too?'

Humans often find animal companions who resemble them in some way. I'd always imagined that, if my dad found himself reflected back from the animal kingdom, it would be in the form of something untameable, stubborn, excitable. I'd been thinking in terms of a black rhino, perhaps, or an unusually attention-happy elk, not so much of a kitten barely bigger than his own foot.

Here, though, was the undeniable evidence. Passed out together there on the sofa, they even *looked* sort of similar: two soulmates, their batteries run down in perfect accordance after a day of boundless energy, dizzying enthusiasm and full-throttle anecdote.

In theory, I should have been ecstatic. I'd been campaigning for years for an extra, part-time cat that I could visit in the Midlands, and now I'd got him. More than that, Floyd was brilliant in every way I could have reasonably hoped for: entertaining, energetic *and* cuddly. But there was a 'be careful what you wish for' element to all this. Over the last few weeks, I'd been informed that Floyd was the best cat ever at – amongst other things – sleeping, fetching, meowing, eating, jumping, dancing and cuddling. I didn't begrudge any of this, but it did put Roscoe's progress into perspective. Every week brought a new, entertaining discovery about her talents, but she was growing into a much more independent, aloof cat than Floyd. This independence and aloofness only increased a few weeks later when she was spayed and began to go out, unaccompanied, for the first time. If you saw Roscoe – whether inside the house or, especially, outside – there was always a sense that she was on the way to a meeting, or some other important cat business. She might stop and give you a quick high five, but she had places to be, people to see.

'Can you remember when we had a kitten?' Gemma would ask, as our first summer with Roscoe went on.

'Yes, that was nice, wasn't it?' I'd reply. 'We should get another one some time.'

Roscoe had warmed to Gemma far more quickly than she'd warmed to me. I'd hoped that would be the case, but she had made it clear that she was not a cat who would brook the neediness of any human who happened to be in a vertical position. She received affection in a much more fleeting, casual way than Ralph, Shipley or The Bear did. She was, like Floyd, a little doglike, at least in the sense of her reactions to a stroke or a scritch: she enjoyed them in a happy and carefree manner, but there was no sense that she was experiencing any great, intense pleasure from it. She always made it clear that there would soon be other matters to take care of elsewhere. I'm not sure what these matters were, but I tended to picture an evening job in social media, or putting her cartoonish looks to good use by modelling for a cat food company.

A continuing exception to the 'no strings attached' rules of Roscoe's affection were the occasions when Gemma and I were wrapped in a towel. Roscoe loved towels so much that, were you merely holding one, she would follow you around the house in the hope that you might pause and let her attach herself to it in some way. This made for some very rewarding moments of bonding, but would have been inconvenient on a full-time basis. Because I kept rather odd working hours, I already answered the door to my local postmen and women in a variety of garments; were they to see me clad only in a large John Lewis bath sheet, I sensed they would view it as the final evidence confirming their suspicions that I was not a hardworking writer at all but a layabout who smoked weed all day in his underclothes whilst playing Mortal Kombat.

Like people, some cats just seem to feel stuff on a deeper level than others: it's a predicament with its pros and cons. On the plus side, as a free and easy kind of kitten who didn't seem to let much bother her, Roscoe was completely accepting of Ralph, Shipley and The Bear. Those first few antagonistic, constipated days were thankfully an anomaly. Like many cats, and humans, Roscoe seemed a little in awe of Ralph's magnificent physical presence, often following him around and sliding up against him – mostly to his beaming approval, only occasionally to his faint irritation. Her relationship with The Bear was more distant, but mutually tolerant – as if the two of them knew that they came from such different worlds that they couldn't possibly clash. The only hint of aggro came between her and Shipley, since she continued to delight in getting right up into his face. Shipley's petulance – his curses now sounding like a protest along the lines of 'It's my role to be annoying – this isn't allowed!' – only encouraged her. His attempts to subjugate her with violence were always restrained, and she remained completely fearless of him.

Her true nemesis remained her doppelgänger in the bedroom mirror. For periods of up to an hour, the two of them would stare each other out, wondering who was going to make the first move. Finally, Roscoe would decide to put an end to all this by going behind the mirror to find the impostor and punish her, only to discover that she had scarpered. Ralph occasionally checked out his reflection – which was entirely understandable, to anyone who had seen what Ralph looked like – but on the whole, my other cats appeared fairly oblivious to mirrors and televisions. Roscoe's sharp, clear button eyes, however, seemed to pick out the action in them. She would frequently spend lengthy periods gazing up at whatever film or TV show Gemma and I were watching, every so often moving forward to attack the screen with a paw. I'm not sure how much of the action she could follow, but her taste seemed to be impressively discerning. She particularly loved golf coverage, and I was proud when she reached up to casually assault the American journeyman pro Brandt Snedeker, whose businesslike style of play never really excited me. Similarly, while she seemed to appreciate Mark Wahlberg's excellent performance alongside Christian Bale in *The Fighter*, she understandably snapped after watching him for three-quarters of an hour in the severely substandard *Contraband*, giving his two-dimensional face what can only be described as a 'paw smackdown'.

With Roscoe now infertile, there were no worries about what one of the occasional male feral visitors to the house could do to her future, and ours. That said, Alan had taken a bit of a shine to her recently, and his forays into the house were greeted in a less serene manner by Ralph, Shipley and The Bear than they once had been. Deborah had told me that he'd pissed in one of her favourite boots a few weeks ago, so I should probably not have been surprised at his habit of urinating on my records in the exact same spot as Graham. Still, there was something a bit disheartening about it. It just wasn't the kind of thing you expected an Alan to do. More troubling still, The Bear was once again following suit, with Bill Withers taking a hammering that even he might have considered harsh. The 1976 album *Naked and Warm* had come off particularly badly, and probably wished it wasn't quite so naked, or so warm.

Maybe this was just The Bear's and Alan's way of telling me that nobody really *needed* to own eight Bill Withers albums, but I decided it was time to take action. I'd signed a mental contract with myself when I decided to live with multiple cats. This contract included the condition that, if I was going to be so indulgent as to let several furry urine machines share my house, I would not, on any account, ever become The Person Whose House Smells of Wee and Who Doesn't Know It. For that reason I'd always been scrupulously clean, but there comes a point – if you have ferals, or ex-ferals, in the neighbourhood – where kitchen roll, cloths and disinfectant are no longer enough.

I'd considered magnetic catflaps in the past, but had been put off by reports of magnets falling off collars, and cats turning up in houses with strange keys and coins stuck to their necks. 'I wouldn't get one if I were you,' my

aunt and uncle had told me. 'We did, and we kept finding the cats stuck to the fridge.' A microchip catflap,
however, was by all accounts a good bet. If I'd put it off,
it was perhaps due to some last fleeting hope that
Graham would return, but there'd been no sign of him
for almost three months now, and Gemma and I had
finally faced up to the fact that he was gone for ever.
The microchip flap did not necessitate adding anything
unwieldy to the cats' neck areas, and all the cats were
already chipped. It would just be a matter of getting the
flaps themselves, and programming in the details of the
cats' chips.

I was thinking about more than just cleanliness here.
In August we'd had a small health scare involving The
Bear on his visit to the vet's to get his latest flea treatment (the injection he was required to have due to his
allergy to normal flea treatments). 'He's lost a little
weight,' said the locum vet, in an extremely strong
Welsh accent. 'Has he been eating much?'

I told him that The Bear had been eating more than
ever recently.

'Hmmm,' said the vet. 'It could be worth getting his
thyroid checked out.'

A nervous twenty-four hours followed, all the more
troubling for its echoes of Janet. The Bear was given the
all-clear, but the experience served as a bit of a jolt to the
picture I'd built up of him as a cat who grew more youthful with age. Because The Bear was delicate and polite
and elderly, I went the extra mile to make sure he was
comfortable in so many areas of his day-to-day life,

allowed him little privileges that I didn't always allow Ralph, Shipley and Roscoe. I decided that it was the least I could do to include among these comforts a sense that his territory was not being invaded by strange cats. Additionally, I concluded that the microchip flaps would be an investment for the future, when robots took over the earth and I needed a device to let nice robots into my house but keep out evil, feral ones.

I did consider attempting to fit the flaps – which came from a company called Sureflap – myself, but in retrospect I'm glad I didn't. The first handyman I paid to install them half-fitted one, leaving it partially hanging out of the wall, mounted on a piece of wood he appeared to have found in a bin, then left, seemingly on the verge of tears, shaking his head and muttering the phrase 'I tried to make it good'. After that, I never saw him again. I was beginning to think the brand name of the flap was less a reference to the solidity of the apparatus than to the state that the person dealing with it was likely to get into, but a couple of weeks later, a burly, shaven-headed man in his fifties called John came along and very calmly rectified the damage. I would have pegged him for a dog man, but, as I wrote out a cheque for him, he told me he was a lifelong cat lover. 'That one watched me the whole time,' he said, pointing out The Bear. 'He seemed very interested.'

'Oh, yes, he'll do that,' I said.

'I stopped to give him a cuddle at one point. He really holds on tight, doesn't he? I don't think I've ever felt anything like that from a cat before, and I've known a lot of cats. He has this way of looking at you. Like he's been here before. Like he knows stuff. I don't mean in a bad way, though. I mean in a kind way, in a good way.'

With a Sureflap, all you have to do is put some batteries in, pop it into memory mode and pass a cat through the flap a couple of times, so it memorises the code on their chip. If I ever read the instructions that come with products, I would have known this, but I don't. Instead, before I tried the flap out, I took all the cats to the vet's, in two separate journeys, to be scanned by a new Norwegian vet, so I could get their code, which I'd assumed I'd have to program into the flap by hand. Rightly, the cats seemed to view this as a faintly ridiculous exercise, and surely would have told me of my idiocy had they been able to speak.

Fortunately, the fiasco surrounding the catflaps ended there, and, when they actually began working, there were no real hiccups. That is, if you overlook the first day, where Ralph stood outside the bottom floor flap meowing his own name, and several days after that, where Roscoe didn't seem to be able to get it into her head that she wasn't supposed to open the flaps backwards, using one of her paws. About a week after that, I saw just how effective the flaps were, as, from the living-room window, I watched Ralph shoot into the downstairs flap, then Alan attempt to enter behind him, only to be denied, like a driver who'd tried and failed to cheat a parking barrier by tailgating the car in front.

I imagined those two gossiping ferals again, meeting by the compost heap at the bottom of the garden to discuss this latest development.

'So that's it, then: the end of an era.'

'I'm telling you: this is the way society's going now. Computers are taking over. Soon there won't be any jobs for real, honest cats, defending their territory.'

'Since when were you a real, honest cat?'

'OK, but still. It's sad, y'know. A sign how things are changing.'

'I heard Black Whisker Ed was heading over from Framlingham tomorrow. He's going to be well pissed off when I tell him we're postponing the Cat Skins party.'

'Rather you than me.'

'I'm going to miss fighting behind those curtains in the living room. I reckon in time we'll look back at it as our own equivalent of the golden age of the illegal rave.'

I inspected the job that John had done on the bottom flap. It was a neat one. He had 'made good', as builders liked to say. Just a few feet away, the hole in my conservatory roof had opened up again. Above it was a fence badly in need of paint, and a garden gate that had come off its hinges. Carry on around the corner and back into the house and you would find sofas decimated by claws, a scuffed floor that more houseproud people might have resanded and varnished three or four years ago, and a small hole in a wall, through which two slugs eagerly poked their heads. Head back downstairs, past chewed carpets, and outside again, and you saw a shed, now missing its door, and leaning so far into next door's garden that it had ceased to resemble a broken shed and taken on the appearance of an abstract art project. 'If you ever decide to put this place on the market, please remember to tell me,' said John, who clearly had the vision of a man who spends his days ripping things down and remaking them with his hands.

It was something I'd thought about recently, a lot – especially as I knew how much Gemma missed the West Country. If it were to be the case, I'd have to attend to all of these cosmetic matters first. And I planned to, just as soon as my bank account had recovered from the cost of getting two hi-tech catflaps fitted, having one cat tested for hyperthyroidism and injected with grade-one flea protection and two other cats sterilised – one of whom actually lived with me, and one of whom had summarily vanished. It was a matter of priorities. As a place for humans to live, my house had never felt more threadbare and vulnerable. But for cats, it was a bona fide fortress. That was the important thing. Wasn't it?

Keeping our Cats out of the Bedroom: Instructions for Housesitters

1. Dear_____ and _____. Thanks again for doing this. It will make our holiday so much more relaxing to know you are here. We are confident the cats will be in good hands with you, and I doubt they'll cause you any trouble. Just wanted to warn you about one thing: it's absolutely crucial that during your stay you keep all four of the cats out of the bedroom. The old intellectual black one pissed on the curtains a while back, then the middle-aged mouthy black one pissed in the same place to wind him up. And, even though I've washed the curtains thoroughly several times since then and they smell lovely now, you know how it is: once a cat's pissed on some curtains, that cat will never really forget that those curtains are a lovely place to piss.

The narcissistic tabby one and the small black and white one who looks like a living cartoon aren't interested in pissing on the curtains, but they do love to bounce all over the bed when their paws are muddy. Also, the narcissistic tabby one really likes to meow his own name and the word 'HELLO!' at 3 a.m. You don't want that in the same room as you. Believe me.

2. There is a slight problem with the bedroom door. Even though it's heavy, it doesn't quite click shut properly, which means that the mouthy black one, who is as strong and sinewy as a monitor lizard, can push it open. My method for stopping this from happening used to be to place a very old, large, coverless cushion behind the door, but I don't do that any more, because the old intellectual black one did something unspeakable to it. Also, don't even think about using that sausage-dog-shaped 1970s draught excluder. It's useless. I don't know why I bought it really. I suppose when you're hung over and you're out shopping with friends, stuff like that can seem like a good idea, but you often regret it. Try using one of the massive heavy cushions off the sofa instead.

Also, if you're passing the big secondhand shop on Magdalen Street in Norwich, maybe you could drop the sausage-dog draught excluder in there for me? Ask for Eric. He's the one with the limp who looks like he used to be in The Hollies.

3. If the mouthy black one is feeling particularly determined, he can still push the door open, even if one of the massive heavy cushions from the sofa is behind it, especially on nights when he's waded through the fen up the road and wants somewhere soft to wipe his paws. As he does so, he'll normally make a very loud sweary noise, a bit like a disgruntled teenager, but also slightly like an angry pterodactyl. Don't worry, though: this only happens twice a week on average, and it's manageable. You just have to keep one eye constantly open and be ready to leap out of bed and intercept him before he spreads peaty jet-black muck all over the duvet and my original 1970s Superman pillowcase.

4. Sometimes, when the mouthy black one breaks in and you're trying to intercept him, the small black and white one who looks like a living cartoon will nip in after him and scurry under the bed. Try not to concern yourself too much with her. She's very hard to catch and the worst she'll do is attack your feet in the night or burrow into your stomach as if it contains a treat that, with enough probing, she thinks she will be able to find and eat. Most probably she'll just head into the bathroom next door and fall asleep on the folded towels. Make sure that before using it you remember to wash the towel she's

slept on, though – and perhaps the one underneath it, just for insurance. When you carry the towel to the washing machine, she will probably follow you, with a slightly unnerving, eager look on her face.

5. The old intellectual black one does sometimes have night terrors. I probably should have mentioned that earlier. Please don't be alarmed by these. They normally involve him walking around the kitchen making a weird wobbly-lipped noise which sounds like he has seen the ghost of a deceased lover or is questioning the very nature of existence. I probably make that sound worse than it is. The narcissistic tabby one, for example, is far, far louder when he walks around meowing his own name or ticking cat jobs off a small invisible cat clipboard. The old intellectual black one won't trouble you for long – maybe forty-five minutes at the most. Pop in there and give him a cuddle if possible. He's used to that, and he might feel even more alone and scared without it.

6. Of course, while you're on a separate floor of the house, comforting the intellectual black one, there's also the possibility that the mouthy black one will take advantage of your absence and break into the bedroom, followed by the small black and white one who looks like a living cartoon, and the narcissistic tabby one, who

does, I should probably say, have a small problem with bringing slugs in on his back at the present time. If so, you can't be blamed, and maybe it will be best to abandon the bedroom altogether. You don't want to be waking up later with bits of soil or slugs between your toes, and, in the words of a couple of my friends who have stayed over recently, 'That sofa bed is almost as comfortable as some real beds!' Don't worry. It's no big deal. Have a fantastic stay and we'll see you in just over three weeks!

P.S. If you visit the farm museum up the road, make sure you get some fudge from the shop. It's excellent.

It's Ralph's World –
The Rest of Us Just Live in It

Taking into account that the seventies was such a loud decade, in terms of music and politics and fashion, there's something surprisingly *quiet* about the generation born during it. People born in the seventies – or 'Generation X', as we're sometimes called, when it's convenient – have neither the massive strength in numbers nor the cultural explosion of the baby boomers to define them. Nor do we have the 'in your face' element of Generation Y. Yet what comes after Generation X – what every Generation X-er has to deal with, and will almost certainly have something to say about, if you speak to them at any length – is arguably the most significant generation gap of the last century: that between people who grew up with the Internet, and people who didn't.

Because I was born in 1975, it means I am one of the

last group of people able to remember the time when men and women would go on nights out without any thought of taking photos of one another, when an answerphone was largely considered a luxury that only posh people had, when arranging to meet someone meant trusting that they'd be there at the time you'd agreed upon and waiting a while then going back home if they weren't, when pornography was something mainly found high on a newsagent's shelf or torn up and strewn, inexplicably, across the countryside not far from my house. It also means I can remember a time when being a cat lover was very different.

Cats have been all over the Internet for many years. This makes total sense, as they seem to spend half their lives trying to stand and sit on the keyboards of our laptops. For a cat lover, though, it's a bit of a double-edged sword. There's the wonder of having access to innumerable funny cat videos and being able to share your love of cats with other ailurophiles around the world. At its best, it can be very creative – like a more sophisticated version of ancient Egypt, with LOLcats and viral potentiality instead of hieroglyphs. (And who knows? All history is distortion. Maybe the Egyptians didn't actually worship cats but just liked to share stupid pictures of them, and stuff got exaggerated over time?)

Yet, at the same time, the sheer overkill of cat-related memes – and, for all the great cat-related content, there is no doubt that a huge amount of it is mawkish, repetitive, platitudinous rubbish – has turned 'cat' into a dirty word for many Internet users: something lowbrow that gets in the way of the real issues of social net-working, such as telling people what you had for breakfast, upping the ad revenue of the *Daily Mail* by posting outraged links to its articles, or arguing with a complete stranger about whether or not you tweet too much. Cats, no doubt, would be disgusted at being branded as lowbrow. They'd also surely be very dis-heartened about the sad knock-on effect of cat meme overkill, which is the fact that – especially if you're female – a love of cats, and a domestic set-up where sev-eral of them are present, has to many people become synonymous with the state of having no life, and few romantic prospects.

When I was growing up in the 1980s and 1990s, most women I knew had cats. I don't remember that it signi-fied anything other than that they liked cats, and were probably quite kind and nice. Certainly, I saw a couple of people who had more cats than was healthy either for them or the cats, but that didn't seem anything to do with the fact that the animal they were projecting their unhappiness onto was feline: they could just as easily have been living with too many weasels or parrots.

Nowadays, though, Crazy Cat Lady is entrenched in our psyche. Like all stereotypes, there's a grain of truth to her, but she's a million times more present in that flip-pant but damaging thing 'Internet banter' than she ever could be in real life. Jokes about Crazy Cat Ladies seem harmless enough, but at their core is a disturbing echo of the hysterical witch superstitions of the late Middle Ages. I've known several women who have wanted to get a cat, or an additional cat, but have hesitated, or decided not to, because of 'what it might say about them'.

Personally, I'd like to see Crazy Cat Lady's name never mentioned again: for the good of male–female relations, for the good of feminism, for the good of human self-esteem, for the good of cats – particularly rescue cats. That's clearly not going to happen, though, so instead a large faction of women have started embracing the Crazy Cat Lady title as a subversive way of drowning out the negative assumptions that go with it. In 2009, you might not have seen 'Crazy Cat Lady, and proud of it' in many Twitter biogs, but by 2012 it had become far more common, along with a flaunting of cat tattoos and cat-related furniture and clothing. This not just from single, childless women over the age of thirty-five, but from women of all ages and appearances, in many different careers, with varying romantic statuses.

Admirable as this proud attempt to turn the tables is, and support it though I do, I'm not sure if I'd be bold enough to join in, if I were of the opposite gender and had been put in the Crazy Cat Lady box. I think the chief problem is, as much as I love cats, I don't love many cat-related *things*. It's another stipulation of my contract with myself as a cat owner. I've got two T-shirts with cats on them: one was sent to me by a cat charity I supported, and the other was bought as a present, less because it had a cat on it and more because it was funny. I don't have any cat jumpers, or an armchair with a cat print on it. I currently have some form of drawing or sculpture of a hare in every room of my house, yet I only have one cat-themed wall hanging: a montage of photographs of an upside-down Janet, to remind me what an adorable nutcase he was.

I've never seen the musical *Cats* and have no desire to do so. I accept that friends and family will often send me birthday cards with drawings or photos of cats on them, but I'm always quietly pleased when they opt for another theme. A reader of my first book on cats once sent me three tiny cardigans as presents for The Bear, Ralph and Shipley, each with an individual name tag, and, feeling I'd be somewhat ungrateful not to, I started coaxing each of them to try them on. But I found myself stopping in the middle of the process, feeling rather uncomfortable about it. The way I view my cats is not that they're a hobby, or child substitutes, but a bunch of friends who just happen to be smaller and furrier and more self-obsessed than most of my other friends. There are certain things you do with friends, and certain things you don't. Will and Mary, for example, are friends, but I don't feel compelled to get a tattoo on my arm dedicated to them, or hang framed woodcuts of their faces all over my house.

My slight aversion to items featuring cats meant that, by my mid-thirties, I had seen what many cat aficionados might have viewed as a pitiful number of films from the feline canon. I'd watched the original 1942 film noir version of the horror movie *Cat People*, but that's probably clutching at straws. 1988's *Heathcliff: The Movie*, 2001's *Cats and Dogs* and 2004's *Garfield: The Movie* had always been way off my radar.

One day in late summer 2012, I came upstairs from my office to find Gemma singing to The Bear, 'Ev'rybody wants to be a cat.'

'That's a nice song,' I said. 'Did you make that up?'

'You're kidding me, right?'

'No. It's nice. I mean it.'

'Surely you know that song. It's from *The Aristocats*. The Disney film.'

'Nope. Never seen it.'

'But everyone's seen that film.'

'Not me. Is it good?'

I could have said this was perhaps another small measure of the gap between me, as someone born in the seventies, who'd grown up with only three channels of kids' TV, and Gemma, a member of the more culturally saturated generation below me. In truth, the main reason I hadn't seen *The Aristocats* was that I'd spent most of my childhood outside, riding my bike or playing football or golf. I sensed, though, from Gemma's review and a few I read on the Internet, that if I was going to watch one film about cats, I could do a lot worse.

As luck would have it, that weekend *The Aristocats* happened to be on TV, and five of us – Gemma, me, Shipley, Ralph and The Bear (but not Roscoe, who'd seemed a bit anti-films ever since her attack on Mark Wahlberg during *Contraband*) – sat down to watch it. Shipley only lasted about five minutes before wandering off swearing, and The Bear bowed out at around the airing of the theme song, apparently in disagreement at its generalisations (not *everyone* wanted to be a cat – The Bear obviously didn't want to be a cat; he wanted to be a poet, or a diplomat), but the rest of us lasted the course, and I surprised myself by quite enjoying it.

The story revolves around a mother cat called

Duchess and her three kittens, who belong to the wealthy former opera singer Madame Adelaide Bonfamille. Had she existed in the Internet age, Madame Adelaide might have been branded a Crazy Cat Lady, and perhaps gone on to write self-abasing confessional pieces about her life in the *Daily Mail*, but this is 1910, so she's just a somewhat eccentric old lady. Learning that Adelaide's cats will inherit her fortune when she dies – but that in the event of their death, the money will pass into his hands – her evil butler Edgar drives Duchess and her kittens into the remote French countryside and releases them. Here they meet Thomas O'Malley, a con-man Lothario moggy from the wrong side of the tracks with a good heart, who shows amazing restraint around Duchess, given that he is attracted to her and clearly hasn't been taken to the vet's to have his balls cut off by interfering strangers. We learn that O'Malley is an alley cat, which seems a little strange, as the area of rural Burgundy where he happens upon Duchess and her kittens has a notable dearth of alleys. Soon, though, they are all making their way back to Paris to avenge the wrong that has been done to them, aided by some British geese who are by some distance the most annoying part of the film, and made me look with new fondness upon a particularly stroppy Muscovy duck who'd been spending time in my garden recently.

Ralph sat on my lap the whole way through *The Aristocats*, padding my chest and dribbling lightly in some of the more frantic earlier stages, then falling into a deep, snoring sleep during the climax. Witnessing the high life of Thomas O'Malley, its dalliances with well-bred female cats and its all-night feline jazz parties, I couldn't help looking at Ralph, in his magnificent sideburned glory, and feeling a little wistful about his lot in life. If any of my cats had been a born ladies' man, it was him, yet all I'd done throughout his life was emasculate him. Having been called Prudence for the first few months of his life, by the time he had been given a name becoming of his rugged manliness, he was missing a couple of vital components. This was a necessity, in a world where there are too many unwanted kittens: a straightforwardly responsible act that didn't require any debate, but, with Ralph's looks and irrepressible good nature, it was also a little like slapping God in the face. I couldn't help feeling I'd been slightly cruel: as if I'd gone up to Kurt Russell during his role as MacReady in the 1982 film *The Thing*, stroked his magnificent beard and hair, then gently broken it to him that for the rest of his life he was not allowed to touch a member of the opposite sex.

Oh, there had been love affairs, of sorts, in Ralph's life. During his kittenhood, he'd seemed to idolise Brewer and had fallen into a year-long slump after his death. After that, his attentions had moved in the direction of a sheepskin rug, which he could often be found padding and thrusting on, whilst staring with determination at a distant and invisible, yet apparently very attractive, object. In another heartless gesture, though, I'd recently got rid of the rug. It dated from my previous relationship, and I'd become almost oblivious to it in the last three and a half years, but one day recently I'd caught sight of it and realised: 'I have part of a dead animal in my house. I do not want part of a dead animal in my house.' Additionally, it still had just a trace of Ralph's dried sick on it from 2010 that I could never quite remove.

So what did that leave? There was Shipley, but, although something of a brotherly bond still remained between the two of them, the way Ralph viewed Shipley tended to drift between irritation and indifference. Roscoe had recently got into the habit of attempting to jump on Ralph's back from a variety of lofty surfaces, and he'd weathered this in a fairly mellow manner, but you wouldn't exactly say she was *interesting* to him. Then there were the slugs, but that was a bit of a one-sided romance, too.

'Ralph only really loves you,' Gemma told me, perhaps accurately. I'd hurt Ralph so often in the time I'd known him. There had been the neutering, and the removal of the sheepskin, and the time in his youth I'd thrown an empty cardboard box quite near him in frustration after he'd maimed a heavily pregnant rat and left it on the staircase. To add insult to injury, there were my dietary decisions of the last few years. Now, when he ran to my cereal bowl and food plate to check for leftovers, as his brain had trained him to do, following years of excitement, he found only soya disappointment or leftover falafel woe. Yet Ralph continued to love me. Even though Gemma was around Roscoe, Shipley and The Bear for not much more than half the time that I was, it could be argued that they were as much her cats as mine.

But not Ralph. His enthusiasm for being around me was such that it could virtually be considered that most un-feline of traits: obedience. I now bore the brunt of the sheepskin's absence, many of the softer parts of my body having to withstand the pummelling that it had once endured.

It seemed a shame that Ralph's love could not be more liberally spread around, since he had so much to give. He'd always been a mellow cat, and – if you overlooked the moments when he meowed his own name at the top of his voice – had only grown more mellow with age. Of course, he'd had his ginger-tabby race war with Pablo a while back, and knew how to put Shipley in his place with a nonchalant body slam, but the idea of him growl-ing these days seemed as unlikely as the Dalai Lama suffering from road rage. When Ralph was in a good mood, which was most of the time, he turned the myth-ical grin of the Cheshire Cat into reality. There was always a sense that there was a thought bubble above his head saying 'I know: majestic aren't I?' When he lay in a patch of sunlight, you got the feeling that it was a case of the sunlight finding him, not him finding the sunlight.

But, like any rock star, he had his ego problems and his secret hang-ups. He remained nervous around new people, in a way that Shipley, Roscoe and even The Bear weren't. 'What does this person want from me?' he always seemed to be thinking, when a stranger or semi-stranger came to the house. 'Are they just interested in me for my effortless shaggy good looks and giant side-burns?'

Ralph had also always experienced something of a problem with summer. His relationship with the sun seemed to dance around the line separating love from hate. He loved to recline in a sunspot, but during prolonged periods of heat he could often be found yowling in heavy foliage, as if in pain, or looking dishevelled and glum. I'd come to view it as his own special form of Seasonal Affective Disorder. Since 2012 didn't actually feature a summer, it had turned out to be a good year for him. He could often be found sleeping under the pampas grass, with one eye open, as I gardened, or taking a dust bath in one of the flower beds. One day in early September I was building a fence out of brushwood where a tree had fallen down and came back up the garden with the wheelbarrow to see him sitting happily next to a hedgehog. It was hard to tell from the expression on the hedgehog's face, but I sense that there was nothing accidental about their coupling.

Over the next quarter of an hour, not wishing to butt in on whatever the two of them had going on, I observed them from twenty or so feet away. Whenever Ralph moved a yard or two, so, very quickly afterwards, did the hedgehog. As it did so, Ralph beamed, in his best 'I didn't ask to be beautiful' way. I'm not sure if the hedgehog beamed too, or even if it's possible for hedgehogs to beam, but it didn't seem unhappy with the situation. I had a closer look at the hedgehog and it had a few ticks stuck to it, which I assumed might have been a bonding point, given Ralph's history with parasites. As if to confirm this, Ralph reached up a paw and gave his neck a violent scratch, but the hedgehog didn't flinch. It was nice to see the way the two of them seemed able to be totally themselves around one another, without any need to put on any airs or graces or pretend to be better than they were.

I went inside to fetch the hedgehog a saucer of milk, vaguely remembering the time – probably in 1986, or 1987 – when my mum and dad had fed the same thing to a hedgehog that their friend Jean had accidentally stepped on outside our back door. By the time I came back, though, the hedgehog was gone. As it transpired, this was a good job, since I soon found out that hedgehogs are dangerously lactose intolerant. It turned out that 'it's good to feed hedgehogs milk' was one of those misguided bits of folk wisdom I had been told as a child in the eighties, along with 'Cats on the continent prefer to be stroked backwards' and 'Girls like you more if you use hair gel'. Milk could in fact be considered one of hedgehogs' main enemies, alongside slug pellets, badgers and cars.

As someone who lives in the British countryside, it's easy to take hedgehogs for granted. If you'd never heard of hedgehogs and you saw one in your garden, you'd probably run up to the next human you saw, grab them furiously by the lapels and tell them that some kind of apocalypse was coming, but because we see them so often, we tend to think 'Oh look – a creature entirely covered in needles who lives in the undergrowth: how normal' instead. They'd always seemed like gentle souls to me, victims of the animal world – arguably more likely to strike up a friendship with a cat like The Bear than with one of life's ostensible winners, such as Ralph – and, feeling sad that I'd scared this one off, and to learn that their numbers had fallen by twenty-five per cent in Britain in the last decade, I decided it was time I found out more about them.

One surprising detail I learned about hedgehogs is the common belief that the first thing you should do if you see one is weigh it. A hedgehog that weighs under 600 grams – which will usually be one that has been born late, in June or July – might not survive the winter, and needs to be rehabilitated by someone with proper hedgehog knowledge before being released back into the wild. Unfortunately, I'd not known this when I'd seen the hedgehog with Ralph – nor that the fact that it had been out in the open in daylight was a bad sign – and could scarcely have presumed it. Weighing just isn't the first thing on my mind when I see a wild animal. I don't spot, say, a skinny muntjac deer and think, 'RIGHT! Time to get the scales out.' What I tend to think is, 'Maybe this one won't be like all the others, and will come and live permanently in my garden, and let me call it Bruce, or Clive.' But, in the second decade of the twenty-first century, there are a large number of under-weight hedgehogs wandering through the undergrowth of Britain, as industrial agriculture reduces the amount of macro-invertebrate prey available to them. This reduction in prey has meant that their competition with badgers for it has got nasty. Hedgehogs don't tend to run in packs, and would probably find it hard to take down a grown badger even if they did. So – and I realise there aren't many opportunities to make this statement at the present time – the badgers are winning.

Here are a couple of other surprising things I found out about hedgehogs: it's illegal to drive them through the state of Pennsylvania, and the well-known 1980s nature TV presenter David Bellamy sometimes eats them, often accompanied by herbs. I learned the latter in the section about hedgehogs as a roadkill delicacy in Hugh Warwick's definitive hedgehog memoir-cum-bible, *A Prickly Affair*. Warwick also taught me that hedgehogs have been known to scale walls and turn up in people's first-floor bedrooms. Julie, a friend of a friend in Norfolk, who could be found fostering around a dozen hedgehogs at any one time, told me that they can travel up to twelve miles in one night. Warwick puts it at more like four kilometres. Whatever the case, they move more swiftly than many of us give them credit for.

A month or so after Ralph's dalliance with the hedgehog in the garden, I visited Shepreth Wildlife Park in Hertfordshire, which hosts one of the country's biggest hedgehog hospitals, and met its curator, Rebecca Willers. With her hardworking team, Rebecca was researching better ways to care for and understand hedgehogs, including the possibility of fitting them with GPS tracking systems. Underweight or injured hogs – one, tragically, had been the victim of a garden strimmer – were usually brought to Shepreth by thoughtful members of the public. 'One hedgehog arrived here alone in a taxi,' Rebecca told me. 'The driver said the fare was already covered. It had come forty miles, all the way from Watford.'

Rebecca and Julie both emphasised the point that people shouldn't try to turn wild hedgehogs into pets: that their true home is in the wild. When I visited Julie and her hedgehogs at her barn conversion, ten miles or so from my house, she showed me a hedgehog whose spines were half-white, rather than the usual browny-beige. 'It's probably mated with one of the domesticated albino ones people have as pets,' she explained.

Julie's teenage daughter, Jessica – who got the idea of looking after hedgehogs after overhearing a conversation in her local pet shop involving a lady who said she had 'a load of poorly birds and hedgehogs running around her front room' – loves caring for the hogs but, after they've recovered and reached a healthy weight, they go back into the wild. The one exception was George, the hedgehog who lived in Julie and Jessica's garden. George was perfectly at liberty to go elsewhere if he wanted to, but seemed to prefer to stick around.

'We named George after a vet we took him to when he was poorly,' Julie said.

'He's not Californian, by any chance?'

'Who, the hedgehog?'

'No, the vet.'

'Yes. He is, as a matter of fact. He really loves hedge-hogs, too, and knows lots about them. Do you know him?'

I thought back to George the vet's kind, valiant efforts to cure Shipley, and recalled how Gemma and I had cooed his name experimentally at Graham a few months previously. I wondered just how many different animals my neighbourhood supervet now had named after him.

I headed out into Julie's garden with her brother-in-law, Phil, who lived next door, to meet George (the spiny version, not the undervalued zoological genius), but at first he was nowhere to be seen. There was a creature in one of the small, doorless wooden hutches where George liked to sleep, but it plainly wasn't him. For a start, this creature was significantly bigger than any hedgehog I'd ever set eyes on. Second, it was covered in dusty dark grey fur. Third, it was, to all intents and purposes, dead.

Phil's reaction to seeing this creature surprised me, largely because it didn't involve him screaming 'Sodding hell! What the buggery is that? I'm calling a top nature expert this instant.' I mean, I *assumed* it was a rat, but I couldn't quite be sure: it seemed much bulkier than the rats I'd seen Shipley and Ralph bring in. 'Oh, we get ones that are loads bigger than this,' said Phil, poking it with a stick to confirm its crusty deadness.

Thankfully, we found George in his other hutch, curled up safely for the winter. I looked at him and said, 'Ah,' but in the end there wasn't a lot else to do. He was a hedge-hog and, for all the quirks of his species, in this somnolent state he was a lot like other hedgehogs. With that, we headed back inside, leaving him to what appeared to be a blissful sleep, safely away from Pennsylvania, David Bellamy, badgers, main roads, and the kind of fool who might feed him milk or try to cajole him into a romance with a large, unkempt, narcissistic tabby cat.

A week after visiting Julie, I received a text message from her. I was playing the last few holes of a golf course in Bedfordshire at the time and, as my partners, Robin and Pat, lined up their putts, I snuck over to a small stand of trees to give the message proper attention. 'There's a hedgehog that needs picking up and taking to the vet not far from you,' said Julie. 'I can't get over there just now and I was wondering if you are available. She said it's running around her bathroom, making a mess.'

I replied, asking Julie when I needed to be there. She texted back within what seemed like a second of me pressing 'send', announcing that the hedgehog ideally needed picking up within a couple of hours. If the traffic was fairly clear, I could get back to Norfolk from this end of Bedfordshire in just over two hours. Tempting as it was to stride back onto the green, putter in hand, and announce to Pat and Robin, 'I have to go – a hedgehog is in trouble!' I thought it more sensible to decline.

This, I was starting to realise, is how eccentricity works: it's a slow drip, so quiet that you aren't even aware of it as it gradually fills up your personality. Some people are properly unusual when they're young, but nobody is properly eccentric. It takes time for those off-kilter hobbies and affectations you thought might be a bit unusual or fun – wearing a ridiculous hat, for example, or taking a sheep to a pub, or maybe even having a drawing of a hare in every room of your house – to mould themselves to your character and grow extra organisms. There's also something about ageing and the concomitant awareness of the fleeting nature of existence that tends to make you less worried about being ridiculous, and less judgemental about the quality of ridiculousness in others. I remembered how, at fifteen, I'd despaired as my granddad, driving me to a golf tournament, had stopped his car smack bang in the middle of a country lane, directly behind a horse, fetched a spade, which he just happened to have in the car at the time, and shovelled its manure straight into the boot. I couldn't quite imagine myself doing the same thing, but the episode had seemed progressively less embarrassing to me with every passing year. What was to say that, by the time I was seventy, or even sixty, I wouldn't view it as a perfectly normal part of rural driving?

My dad had recently been scheduled to attend a big and rather fancy publishing party in London. He'd never been to an event like this before, and seemed excited, even by his standards. An hour or so after he'd left, I spoke to my mum on the phone. 'He's been really looking forward to it,' she told me. 'He's taken a bag of courgettes from the garden. I told him it might not be a good idea, but you know how he is – he won't listen to anybody.' I laughed, but then I thought back to a scene a few months earlier, when I'd been foraging on the north Norfolk coast and stopped off in Norwich on my way home to visit Boots the Chemist. Upon reaching the counter, I'd realised that my wallet was at the bottom of my bag, which was still full of the day's findings; in order to retrieve it, I had to empty a considerable proportion of them onto the counter.

In a way, we were probably looking here at the same genetic predispositions; the only difference was how far the sense of embarrassment had decayed. First the man in his thirties, visibly fumbling with some wild spinach in a shopping mall in front of a queue of people and a nonplussed sales assistant in an attempt to purchase shampoo and conditioner in the '3 for 2' range. Then the man in his sixties, offering a large, phallic vegetable to a Booker prize-shortlisted author. Finally the man in his seventies, standing behind a horse with a shovel in his hand, a grin on his face and a cringing teenager watching him through a gap between his fingers.

At twenty-five, I probably would have thought the idea of genuinely considering abandoning a golf tournament to drive 100 miles to rescue a stranger's hedgehog a fairly ridiculous one. That was my age when I'd first met The Bear. I remembered the day, because it was a busy and fairly pivotal one. I'd spent the morning writing, probably breaking off to read a couple of humorous email circulars, neither of which were about cats. Then I'd caught the Tube into town from Finsbury Park to meet with the literary agent who had just signed me up after reading the sample chapters of my first book. After that I'd told myself I would do some more writing 'in a café' but, as was so often the case, I actually spent it browsing in secondhand bookshops and record shops. I'd then got a bus to Camden, where I was reviewing a gig in the evening for a newspaper – a gig by a band that lots of people were predicting could be huge at the time, but whose name, if you mentioned it to anyone under the age of thirty now, would draw only a blank look – and meeting the girl I'd just started dating. From there, I'd gone, for the first time, to meet her cats, Janet and The Bear: the cats who would soon take me into a completely different life.

Even back then, The Bear had seemed like an animal with a dark past who'd lived several lives. Now here he was, twelve years later, at seventeen, still by my side. No living soul had spent more time in my company since then, and I'm sure he could tell me a lot more about myself, and how I'd changed, than I could. Sometimes I would look up from my work to find him staring at me analytically, and wonder just how long he'd been sitting there. The Bear always had the most perfect, almost balletic, posture at moments such as these, belying his old bones. He had never been a slack or sloppy cat, but when he assessed you, he almost always sat up in an especially alert manner, back straight, paws meticulously arranged in front of him, as if he didn't just happen to be staring in your direction, but felt he was *doing a job*, and intended to do it well.

He'd been gathering data on human weakness for a long time now. He'd watched me become a tiny bit more rumpled with every passing year, a new crease or wrinkle burgeoning here, a few more hairs lost or gone slightly salty there. Sure, due to the battles he'd had when he was younger – which I was sure were defensive rather than aggressive – his ears looked like they'd been clipped by

an overzealous ticket conductor on the Norwich to
Liverpool Street line, but I couldn't even blame fighting
for my physical deterioration. He'd witnessed my bad
decisions and my good ones. He'd met me while I was
living a very metropolitan life. Maybe he'd known even
then that, ultimately, it was an aberration? He'd seen
me in the middle of the last decade, feeling a little
trapped, a little bruised from a property mishap, and
becoming a workaholic to sustain a life that was more
materialistic than I'd ever really wished it to be. He'd
probably known that the things that would ultimately
make me happy were the same ones that had always
made my family happy: animals, walking, books, music,
nature. I sensed he probably could have told me all this
in advance, but I doubted that, given the ability to speak,
he would. He might even have been able to tell me my
future, but I don't think he'd want to. Because that
would defeat the object, and undermine the value of life.
As John, the lovely chap who'd fitted the microchip catflap, had observed, The Bear did seem to know things,
but he knew them 'in a good way, in a kind way'.

'HOLD ON,' said my dad when I telephoned him a few
days later. 'I'M GOING TO CHANGE PHONES. I
CAN'T HEAR YOU ON THIS ONE. FOOK! THE
KITTEN'S GONE UP THE CHIMNEY.'

'Oh no! Is he OK?'

'THAT'S BETTER. YEAH, HE'S FINE. HE KEEPS

STARING AT IT, THOUGH. HEDGEHOGS, YOU SAY? CAN YOU REMEMBER WHEN I USED TO WORK AT THAT EDUCATIONAL RESOURCE CENTRE. THE TAXIDERMIST THERE WOULD LET BABY HEDGEHOGS RUN ALL OVER THE STAFF ROOM. YOU'D OFTEN FIND ONE ON YOUR CHEESE SANDWICH. NEXT DOOR'S DOG'S BEEN IN AGAIN.'

I knew by now that, for every story I told my dad about an animal, he would have another, much weirder one with which to upstage me. Cats had been the one exception to this rule in the past, but since the advent of Floyd, I no longer even had that on my side. As Floyd had grown, he'd only become more of a match for my dad's irrepressible energy and propensity for rule-breaking. My mum had banned Floyd from the bedroom, due to his habit of tipping the bin over, spreading mud over the bed and eating bits of her sewing equipment, but she would often find him and my dad in there taking an afternoon nap together. 'I've got this thing that I do when Floyd's naughty, like when he steals the shower plug. I put my finger on his nose and say "No!",' she had told me. 'I've actually started doing it to your dad too now.' I couldn't quite see myself doing the same thing, but I did think back to the time, a couple of years earlier, when my dad had broken my shower by turning the temperature dial too violently, and wondered if, with this method in place, everything might have been different.

'How did the courgettes go down at the party?' I asked my dad.

'PEOPLE SEEMED TO LIKE THEM, BUT THEN I DROPPED THEM ON THE GROUND. THE PARTY WAS OUTDOORS, SO IT WAS VERY DARK WHERE I DROPPED THEM. IT WAS OK, THOUGH, BECAUSE I'D BROUGHT MY HEADTORCH. ARE YOU GOING OUT TONIGHT? IF YOU ARE, WATCH OUT FOR FOOKWITS AND LOONIES. AND NUTTERS. ESPECIALLY NUTTERS, IN FACT. THIS WEATHER BRINGS THEM ALL OUT.' I looked out of the window: it was an overcast, but reasonably pleasant autumn day of middling temperature. I was about to ask what it was about this weather that brought nutters out, but he'd moved on. 'I JUST HAD A WEE AND THE KITTEN CAME INTO THE BATHROOM AND JUMPED UP ONTO THE TOILET AS I DID AND NOW IT'S GOT WEE ON ITS EAR.'

I searched my artillery of recent Roscoe incidents for something to match this, but found nothing. She'd been pretty aloof recently: utterly delightful in the process, but mostly just getting on with her own business. I had seen one gap where we might have got one up on Floyd, in that his meow was so far virtually non-existent. 'Oh, Roscoe has the most amazing meow EVER,' I'd been hoping to be able to tell my mum and dad, but it wasn't quite coming on as quickly as I'd hoped.

'Have you learned to meow properly yet?' I'd asked her the previous week, as she trotted into the kitchen, requesting food.

'Eeeagreowweh,' she'd replied.

A simple 'no' would have sufficed, but I tried to look

at it in a 'meow half full' way: at least she was making an effort.

But, perhaps, in one sense, I was winning the Kitten War. As she passed into adolescence, Roscoe was causing us relatively little trouble. She was out a lot, and seemed vaguely embarrassed by my or Gemma's presence at any time we were in the garden, but that was normal teenage stuff. As Floyd grew, all the energy that had been so sweet when he'd been the size of a girl's ankle boot became more of a liability. Several more household objects had become casualties of his attentions since I'd last seen him – including my mum's computer printer, whose paper tray he'd broken by jamming his paw into it – whereas Roscoe had cost Gemma and me nothing in breakages for several months. Floyd had already slaughtered his first couple of birds, confirming the fears that had made my mum and dad so apprehensive about getting a kitten in the first place, while Roscoe remained kill free. Roscoe had filled out slightly, particularly on her bottom half, but it was obvious that she would not become a big cat. Floyd, by contrast, was thundering towards giant bruiser status, visibly gaining a few inches every time I saw him. What kind of mayhem would he cause when he finally hit full size? Maybe a more pertinent question was: What kind of mayhem *wouldn't* he cause?

'He keeps hurtling through the catflap and breaking the door,' said my mum. 'He's completely hyperactive. I feel like I need to cut out the E numbers in his food. If he was human, he'd be all red and sweaty all the time.'

'HE'S TURNED FROM A FLUFFY BALL OF FUN

INTO A TYPICAL SEX-CRAZED TEENAGER, OBSESSED WITH LICKING HIS OWN GENITALS,' added my dad.

Mercifully, Floyd had been neutered by now. 'HE CRIED WHEN THE VET WAS CHECKING HIS NUTS,' my dad had said. 'I SAID TO HIM "I DON'T KNOW WHAT SHE'S DOING TO YOU, FLOYD, BUT I'M GLAD IT'S NOT ME".' With the knowledge that Floyd was now a eunuch, though, came another fearsome question: How big and hyperactive would he be now if he *hadn't* gone under the knife?

The main victim of Floyd's boisterous ways was Casper. My mum had felt awful in Floyd's early weeks in the house, seeing Casper's forlorn ghost face peering in at the kitchen window, but the two cats had soon become friends, wrestling and grooming one another on a daily basis, and sleeping in a fashion that Gemma – who had always insisted that cats had distinguishable upper and lower limbs, just like humans – called 'arm in arm'. Early on, there seemed to be a big element of hero worship to this from Floyd's side, but as he'd grown, he'd turned into the dominant party. Casper suffered his lusty attacks with complete equanimity, never complaining, and always retaining a beatific facial expression that would have given even Ralph a run for his money.

There's a photo of me with Floyd, taken on Christmas Eve 2012. Gemma called it a 'Cat Whisperer' photo. I'm not sure that such a person as a Cat Whisperer could truly exist (far more likely to exist would be a Human Whisperer: a cat with his own TV show on which he whispered stuff like 'I own your soul' to misbehaving humans), but I can see what she was getting at. Floyd is on my mum and dad's sofa, looking fairly laid back and pleased with the way life is treating him, and I'm leaning over him, appearing to pass some covert information into his ear that might help him in his future endeavours as a cat. In truth, what I was actually telling Floyd at the time was 'Santa Claus is not real'.

I know: it seems cruel. But I worried about Floyd, and I felt it might be time for him to learn some of the harsh facts of life, purely for his own protection. People said that my cats had a perfect life, but compared to his, it was as if they were doing a strict period of feline community service. He had a pliant best friend and owners who were completely under his paw. On tap, he had only the finest quality wet food. He lived well away from main roads, surrounded by tasty walking and flying snacks. When he trotted outdoors, he was encircled by tall, exciting trees, and would begin each day by bolting to the top of one of them. As if all that wasn't enough, my mum and dad's postwoman kissed him on the nose every morning. His life might carry on being wonderful, but it was unlikely to ever be quite this Utopian ever again. I was glad that The Bear had never gone to live with my mum and dad and subsequently had to make the acquaintance of Floyd, as I think he would have found him a touch on the rambunctious side. But at the same time, Floyd could have benefited from the presence of an elder statesman such as The Bear who could pass on a bit of wisdom and explain that he should use his nine lives wisely.

I noticed that, on the track leading to my mum and dad's house, was a new sign that my dad had crafted, in the shape of a cat, for any drivers who happened to be passing. 'PLEASE DRIVE SLOWLY,' it read. 'CATS PLAYING IN TWITCHELL. thank you.'

In my head, I read the capitalised bits of the sign in my dad's voice and the 'thank you' bit in my mum's. 'You've done a really good job with that,' I told my dad. 'But what if you get people who aren't from around here driving down the twitchell and they don't know what twitchell means?'

'EVERYONE KNOWS WHAT TWITCHELL MEANS.'

I liked his idealism, but I wasn't convinced that it tallied with reality. Having grown up in Nottinghamshire, I would like nothing better than to think that the whole world referred to a narrowish rural path between hedges or buildings as a twitchell or, at worst, a jitty. (In fact, if we were being strictly accurate, Thomas O'Malley from *The Aristocats* should have been referred to as a twitchellcat, not an alleycat.) But I knew, from my travels, that there were strange folk who thought otherwise, believing such a passageway to be called a 'ginnel' or a 'twitten' or a mere 'path'.

'ANYWAY, I'M NOT GOING TO CHANGE IT NOW,' said my dad. 'IT'S A SIGN WARNING DRIVERS TO BE CAREFUL AROUND CATS. IT DOESN'T NEED TO BE EDITED FOR POPULIST APPEAL.'

Casper had snuck through the door when we'd returned to the kitchen, and I leaned over, unthinkingly, and fed him one of the anchovies my mum had left out on the table.

'DID YOU JUST GIVE THAT CAT ONE OF THOSE SMALL FISH? YOU'RE AS BAD AS THAT

PORTUGUESE EXCHANGE KID WE HAD STAY-
ING WITH US WHO PUT YOUR MUM'S
SANDWICHES ON THE ROOF THAT TIME.'

Floyd arrived in the kitchen and leapt onto Casper's
back, then proceeded to start biting his neck. I'm an
only child with a smallish family who had never done
Christmas in a big way, but there was something about
having two male cats tenderly humping in the corner of
the room that made the occasion a little more festive.
Gemma and I were spending a second Christmas in suc-
cession apart, due to the logistical difficulties of our
families living in entirely separate parts of the country
and our own home being in another entirely separate
one. Ralph, Shipley, Roscoe and The Bear, meanwhile,
were amusing themselves, with intermittent visits from
Deborah and David. Feeling so spreadeagled – not to
mention broke – at the festive season prompted more
thoughts that it might be time to move on from the
Upside Down House, but I shelved them just for now.
For a start, there were other things to look at, such as
another toad, which had taken up residence in my dad's
running shoe in the porch.

On Boxing Day, my extended family filed in, saying
hello to the toad on the way. I noticed that my cousin
Jack's girlfriend Jade had brought her dog, a chihuahua
called Pom. Floyd had met dogs before – he'd been born
in a house containing a spaniel – but his reaction to
Pom suggested otherwise. We'd been making a cau-
tionary effort to keep the two of them in separate rooms,
but everyone had been a little distracted by my dad's

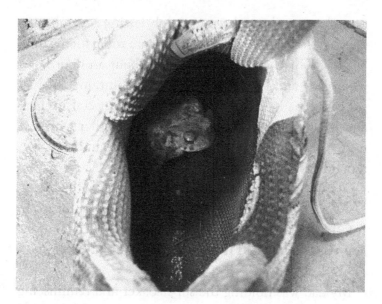

speculations about how difficult it must have been for the toad to make its way along the A14 and the A1 back from my house, and in the meantime, Floyd had snuck into the kitchen. He reacted to Pom in the obvious manner of any small furry creature, meeting for the first time in a room that happens to be full of people a slightly larger furry creature that it is absolutely terrified of: he scrambled on top of a cupboard, then ran at high speed across the tops of the people's heads until he found one with hair big enough for him to hide in.

My cousin Fay used to straighten her hair in her late teens and early twenties, but these days she's at peace with its tight, thick curls and tends to let it grow out with a fair bit of freedom. Disentangling Floyd thus

turned out to be a three-man job lasting several minutes. After that, he sulked in the spare room for a while,
but made his way back downstairs about an hour later,
when Jade and Pom had left. By this point, my dad had
got his new supersoaker out, and he and my cousins Jack
and Jeff were taking turns to spray each other with it. I
noticed that my dad was now wearing a laminated sign
around his neck featuring my uncle Paul's face.

'What's that he's got on?' I asked my mum, quietly.

'Don't ask,' she said. 'It's Paul's security pass for work.
It fell out of Paul's coat when I was putting them away,
and your dad picked it up and put it on. I'm not sure if
Paul's realised yet.'

My dad was holding the supersoaker and reminiscing
about the games of 'Army' that he used to play as a kid
on the street where he lived. 'I USED TO LOVE MY
TOY DAVEY CROCKETT RIFLE BUT SOMETIMES
WE'D ALL JUST USE IMAGINARY GUNS. THE
O'DOHERTYS WERE CRAP AT MAKING THE
SHOOTING NOISES, THOUGH, BECAUSE THEY
COULDN'T AFFORD GOOD IMAGINARY GUNS.
DID I TELL YOU ABOUT THE TIME I CHARGED
ALL MY MATES A PENNY EACH TO SEE A
SQUASHED MONKEY I'D FOUND ON THE
STREET? I FOUND OUT LATER THAT IT WAS
JUST A BIG FROG.'

In recent weeks, according to my dad, a huge, brutish
black cat had been hanging around the garden and
intimidating Casper and Floyd. The supersoaker had
been ostensibly purchased to scare it away, but I was

starting to have my doubts. I'd seen the black cat come in through the catflap on Christmas Day, and Floyd had bounded up to it as if to say 'Hi! I'm Floyd! What's your name? What shall we do NOW!' The black cat didn't seem very impressed, but neither did it look like it was about to start any kind of serious ruckus.

When everyone else had gone home, my dad reluctantly laid the supersoaker down, poured us both a glass of whisky, and I watched an episode of *Dad's Army* with him, just like he'd done at Christmas many times with my granddad. The one difference being that my granddad never had a white and black cat fast asleep upside down on his legs, purring at a volume only slightly softer than most outboard motors. When the episode was over, my dad told a story about the time my grandma had called the police on him for leaving pennies on the railway line, then fell into a deep sleep to match Floyd's. On his hand, I noticed the words 'Potatoes' and 'WASPS!' written in blue ink.

I'd struggled a little bit in the last few years with Christmas presents for my dad. He'd seemed very happy with the whisky and books I usually gave him, but I wanted to be more original. It wasn't easy, though. Most people get harder to buy for as they get older, and if I tried to purchase a gift in one of his specialist areas – gardening, for example, or bebop or doo-wop records made between the years 1944 and 1954 – I'd probably get it wrong or find that he already had it. This year I'd bought him a nicely crafted model of one of his favourite 1950s cars: a result of me making a mental note of a conversation back in spring where my dad had announced, 'IF I WAS RICH ALL I'D DO IS BUY A LOAD OF OLD CARS AND BRUM THEM ALL DAY,' and my mum had replied, 'And not have a wife any more.' I was pretty impressed with myself, but now, looking at him there on the sofa, snoring away with Floyd, I wondered if I'd tried to be too clever. I'd begun to realise in recent years just how brilliant my parents were and was increasingly proud of them. With my dad heading into his mid-sixties, I'd wanted to get him something intricate or unusual to show my gratitude for all the love and support he'd given me over the years, but maybe I just had to face the facts: all he'd ever really wanted for Christmas was a big fake gun and a kitten.

Ten Reasons Why
My Oldest Cat Is Sad

1. My cat is sad because on his travels he has discovered a machine with a face and he now has some concerns he would like to raise.

2. My cat is sad because he never got on the property ladder when he was younger and thinks it might now be too late.

3. My cat is sad because he picked up his housemate's catnip by mistake and it's made of different stuff to his.

4. My cat is sad because of the insufferable
smugness he must deal with every day,
in his line of work.

5. My cat is sad because harsh words have
been exchanged about some of his artwork
and now there is an atmosphere
of tension and regret.

6. My cat is sad because books are sometimes not about what they say they're about.

7. My cat is sad because a female colleague of his has seen a ghost and appears to be very shaken by the experience.

8. My cat is sad because he does not want to make a psychedelic folk rock album with me, or be part of the photoshoot for its cover.

9. My cat is sad because of animal cruelty.

10. My cat is sad because we have only just
started playing Scrabble and already his
luck is down and I am using the game
as a way to hurt him.

Hardy Perennial

There was a time, back around the turn of the millennium, while I was living in London, when I would remain fairly oblivious to the change of the seasons. To a certain kind of overawed, excitable man in his early to mid-twenties who calls a big city home – the kind of man I was at that point – winter, spring, summer and autumn tend to be little more than the gently fluctuating wallpaper behind the really important business of going out to pubs and gigs. If you'd asked me in the year 2000 which colours I associated with different times of year, I might have named, at a push, two: the nondescript grey that signified every point between September and March and the dirty orange that signified the rest.

In Norfolk, however, I not only associate each season with a colour but often mentally assign extra colours to different *parts* of a season. There is, for example, the grainy, spooky charcoal light of early winter. This is very different to the grubby browny-black that sets in two or three months afterwards. By February, Norfolk is usually so caked in mucky residue, you get the sense that if it were a white van, somebody would have written 'Clean me!' or 'I wish my wife was this dirty!' on it with their finger. Sometimes the real miracle of spring in this part of the country seems to be less that everything grows again and more that all that dirt somehow vanishes.

When there's not a hosepipe ban, I do my tiny, inconsequential bit in nature's big clean-up by pressure-washing my balcony and patio. This is the annual job where, in gradual increments, I transfer all the dirt immediately outside my house to my hair, beard, nose and forehead. It takes a long time but, with enough con-centration and effort, by the end I can get myself looking almost exactly like one of the semi-finalists in a bog-snorkelling contest. The pressure washer is very loud, which is why, when Geoff the gardener knocked on my front door in spring 2013, I didn't hear him, despite its close proximity to the balcony, which I was cleaning at the time.

'Thhhffff hh chthhh ghhhhthnnn mnnnnh hhh thhffff dhhhh,' said Gemma, tapping me on the shoulder.

I switched the pressure washer off.

'There's a crazy gardener man at your door,' she repeated. 'He says he's called Geoff and wants to know if we can let him out the back for a look around. I don't know what to say to him.'

I placed the pressure washer's hose attachment on the ground and made a futile attempt to wipe the mud spat-ter off my face. From the window, The Bear, who had been waiting anxiously for his balcony-cum-bachelor pad to be once again available for his use, watched with some curiosity. I racked my brain trying to remember if I'd booked anyone to do gardening work recently. I had the potential to become very forgetful at times like now, when I'd been a bit overworked, but it seemed unlikely that I would have asked for any paid help, given that I currently had a grand total of thirty-seven pounds and sixteen pence in my bank account. Gemma looked a little pale. 'I'm a bit scared,' she said. I thought she might be over-egging things, but upon opening the door, I decided that her reaction to Geoff had, if anything, been an impressively calm one. Five foot eightish, with glasses and a large bushy beard, he wore a stained sweatshirt with the words 'Head Gardener' emblazoned across its front. In case you were still in doubt about his profession, on his head was a baseball cap reading 'Hardy Perennial'.

'Hello!' he said. 'Is this YOUR garden?' As he spoke, he bounced up and down on the balls of his feet, attempting to peer over the fence. 'Do you go in there a LOT?' he continued. 'I bet it's great for sunbathing. Does it go all the way down to the bottom?'

His tone was that of an eight-year-old boy who can't believe his luck to be staying overnight in the room of a ten-year-old with bunk beds. I put him at roughly my dad's age.

'I do a bit of gardening myself,' Geoff went on. 'That's my trade, in fact.' Here he did a double point to his cap and his sweatshirt. 'Do you mind if I come in and have a look around?'

I loved my garden very much. Often, I could scarcely believe my luck in owning it. But I'd also seen many much bigger, tidier, more imaginative gardens, and I was sure someone who worked in the horticulture industry would have seen yet more, so I was surprised at Geoff's enthusiasm. If you were a plumber, it's unlikely you'd spend your day off asking to be let into the houses of people you'd heard had quite nice stopcocks. Obviously, flowers and bushes are more pleasant than the internal organs of a house, but even if overexposure to them had killed none of their mystery, you wouldn't think there'd be any pressing need to seek new ones out during your downtime. That Geoff assured me that he was 'not pitching for work' made his proposal even more intriguing. So, opting to live recklessly in the moment, I opened the gate and led him down to look at my bedding.

'Oh yeah, this is good,' he said, darting down the steps in front of me. 'It's a bit neglected, but it's got potential.' I'd actually been working hard to get the garden up to scratch in recent weeks, chopping down and burning lots of foliage – even going so far as to burn some of next door's by mistake – but I supposed it might look a bit shabby, still, to a professional.

'See that?' said Geoff, pointing behind us to an overgrown bed. 'You want to rake all that debris from that slope and start putting this' – he pointed to my compost heap – 'all over it. Do you mow in horizontal stripes? Do you? Try to do that. It will help. And see these? Cut them off right down here. Near the brown bit. Oh, and you can really lay into that. Don't be scared to be harsh. It will all be back in a month.'

I noticed that The Bear had followed us outside, which was unusual. He'd got a bit slower over the winter, and these days, if he went out at all, he tended to stick to the balcony, or make a sharp left turn out of the bottom catflap in the direction of Biscuit's house. None of the friends who'd been in the garden over the last six months had been sufficiently interesting to tempt him down here, and he'd not even emerged last week when I'd been talking to Deborah over the fence and Biscuit had been milling around her feet, but Geoff had evidently proved too tempting. The Bear sat examining the two of us from ten yards or so, possibly gathering more data for his ongoing analysis of human quirks and foibles.

'Come over here and sit down,' said Geoff, making himself comfortable on a rickety garden bench I'd recently sanded down, and patting the space next to him. 'Is that cat yours? He looks wise. Tell me about yourself.'

As I listened to Geoff's torrent of advice, spluttering only the odd half word or two in response every few seconds, before he moved onto the next bush or bed, I wondered what some of my more cautious acquaintances – those who'd accused me of being 'too trusting' in the past – might make of my current predicament. I had plenty of experience conversing with a loud, excitable man in late middle age, so Geoff's enthusiasm did not faze me, but it suddenly occurred to me that over the last fortnight there'd been reports of a few burglaries in the neighbourhood. Now here I was, trapped on my own property, in the company of a stranger of wild appearance, possibly dangerously under the influence of caffeine, who probably now knew the combination code to the padlock on my gate. In the end, though, I was glad I went with the voice in my head that said Geoff meant well.

'You looked like a couple of wild men sitting out there when I checked on you from the living-room window,' Gemma said later. 'I was a bit worried at first that he was going to hurt you, but it was actually quite cute.'

Geoff, I found out, was a Buddhist. During the eighties, he'd worked as a bank manager in Cambridge but in his mid-forties, after the break-up of his relationship, he'd quit his job and moved to a rented house – 'more of a glorified shed, really' – on the north Norfolk coast, and started working as an assistant to a well-known local gardener. He'd earned a fraction of his previous salary, but was surprised at how little it bothered him. 'You know when you go out on the first sunny day of the year without a coat and you feel really light?' he said. 'It felt like that, but like a much bigger version of it, all the time.'

More recently he'd set up as an independent landscaper. 'I've still got hardly any stuff in my house. A few books. I don't even own a TV. I know I can't take it with me, y'know.' Most of what he ate came from his vegetable garden or his neighbours' chickens.

I noticed that The Bear had not yet moved, save for a brief wander to have a disrespectful wee against Janet's apple tree. There had been an Internet conspiracy theory going around recently claiming that cats were actually aliens, sending information about humans back to their home planet to aid it in taking over our world. I'd had my doubts about this: appraising Ralph and Shipley, they seemed too interested in their own needs to be taking notes on the habits of my species, and Roscoe was just so damn *busy* all the time. Looking at The Bear, though, it didn't seem so far-fetched. Whatever his long-term project was, I felt sure the chance to examine Geoff was aiding his research.

'I'm going to Glastonbury!' Geoff announced. 'Are you going too? Punch that!' he said, lifting up his Head Gardener sweatshirt. 'Go on! Don't be afraid. Punch it!'

I did as he asked. 'It does feel very firm,' I said.

'That doesn't come from the gym, my friend. That comes from walking up and down all day with a wheelbarrow.'

Half an hour ago, I hadn't even known Geoff existed, but now, if anyone had seen us together, they might have thought we were old friends: two dishevelled and hirsute yet reasonably fit men, fooling about on a bench. While I had warmed to Geoff, I was still a little confused by his choice of clothing. As someone who wrote for a living, I took my job around with me on a full-time basis, but it had never occurred to me to wear a sweater with the word 'Author' on it. Perhaps, though, being a gardener was a bigger commitment. Maybe that was why so many horticultural types had names with garden words in them, such as Bob Flowerdew and Alan Bloom. Also, as someone who was wearing a mud-spattered Allman Brothers T-shirt, and whose hair – beaten into submission by wind, water and filth – could be reasonably described as an injury, I was in no position to criticise regarding matters of appearance.

'You say you were born in 1975?' asked Geoff. 'That's the Year of the Rabbit. That means this will be your year! The year it all happens for you. Stuff.'

'Really?' I would have preferred the Year of the Hare, but as that didn't actually exist, I'd take the Rabbit in lieu.

'Oh, no, actually that was the year before last. Sorry.'

'Oh.'

Before Geoff left, he wandered over to give The Bear a scritch under the chin. 'You're the dude, aren't you?' Geoff said.

I'm not sure that The Bear had ever quite considered himself a 'dude' – that was more Ralph's role – but he accepted Geoff's attentions very willingly, and I was once again reminded how much more sociable my oldest cat – now not far from his eighteenth birthday – had become; so distant from that black cloud on legs looking for somewhere to rain who I'd met in London all those years ago. I led Geoff out. He gave me his number on a scrap of paper – a lack of business card was another thing the two of us had in common, to add to beards and a flirtation with Buddhism – and I promised him that, in the rare event that I did find enough money to pay someone to smarten my garden up between now and when I put my house on the market, I would be straight on the phone to him. I honestly got the impression, though, that he hadn't been hustling for work, and just liked meeting new people.

That, then, is what I have decided to do: sell up. It's not been an easy decision, but, in terms of its pull on my time and my finances, the house has been a huge struggle for a long time. A few years ago, I changed it about a bit and made it my own, began to love it and my life with my cats in it a new way, but ultimately, its size and its cosmetic needs were always tailored to a previous life and a more economically stable era for the industry I work in. I can barely remember what that life felt like, and I'm ready for a change, for a domestic set-up that's more relevant to now. Additionally, Gemma misses Devon a lot when she's here, and the 360 miles that separate us when she's not have become more and more painfully palpable.

I suspect I will especially miss Norfolk at this time of year, if I am to leave it behind completely: the way spring seems to erupt here, and the curious human behaviour that often goes with it. We had to wait longer for it than usual this year, which has made its arrival all the more explosive and revelatory. There were times during the biting wind, snow and sub-zero temperatures of early April when I thought the cats might completely lose the plot. You could see them getting progressively more antsy, as if preparing themselves to write a strongly worded complaint to the Weather Board on headed cat notepaper. Shipley's swearing and taunting of The Bear had reached an all-time high, and in late March he took out his frustration on my friends and me by striding into the living room and kicking down a Giant Jenga tower at a crucial moment in the game. Roscoe, meanwhile, seemed frustrated at the number of meetings she'd had to cancel due to adverse transport conditions, and the Bear could be found staring out the window, depressively, his chin flat to the ground.

'RAAAAALLPH!' Ralph would shout, as more snow fell. I heard it as a lament for warmth – the sound of him forgiving summer for all the pain it had caused him in the past – but it was probably just Ralph meowing his own name, as usual.

Now, as The Bear suns his old bones on his balcony, he looks like the pleasure of it is almost too much for him to cope with. '*Thank you,*' he seems to be saying. 'I thought this time would never come.' In the garden, as I continue to tidy up in preparation for marketing the house, Shipley shoots up and down Janet's apple tree, and Roscoe shows me around the place, as if she not only owns it but personally landscaped it: 'This is my apple tree. Over here is my rotting jetty. I often watch ducks from here and try to intimidate them with my still-somewhat-pathetic half meow. I really should get it repaired but I never seem to find a window in my heavy schedule.' She very rarely stays still and, with her white socks, she comes across a bit like a feline version of a fitness freak who is constantly jogging on the spot as she talks to you.

I've agonised so much about taking the four of them

away from all this, because it's hard to picture a place where they could be happier. I'm not sure exactly where we'll go – west, quite possibly – but I would hope that it might be the kind of place where it would not be unlikely for a Buddhist stranger with an amusing sweatshirt to turn up unannounced on your doorstep and tell you his life story. I know The Bear needs his research material, and I will be keeping that in mind. There's still a lot to do before I start househunting in earnest – I imagine getting a shed that doesn't slope at a thirteen-degree angle to the ground could help the sale – but when I do start, one thing is for sure: I'll be thinking about the welfare of the cats as much as Gemma's and my own.

A fortnight ago a letter arrived from the vet: a reminder about a cat booster jab. I opened it hastily, while in the middle of three other jobs, and immediately put it to one side. Only a lot later that day, remembering that all the cats were up to date on their boosters, did I examine it more closely. I zoned out for a moment upon seeing the name, before realising, with a rush of sadness, who it referred to. We'd only called Graham 'Sven' for a short time, but clearly that was the name we'd given to the vet on the day he was neutered and inoculated. Where was he now? Was he still living wild? Had he travelled far away, determined to put as much distance as possible between himself and those who had robbed him of his crown jewels? Had he found another benefactor and learned to trust again? Was he even still alive? These thoughts percolated troublingly in my head for the rest of the day, and the two or three that followed it.

We've had another feral visitor recently: another mournful evening meower imbuing the outside of the house with a ghostly ambience at dusk. Gemma caught site of a flash of ginger in the dark and was convinced for a while it was Graham, but I didn't think the meow had quite the same throaty Rod Stewart quality, and the recent lighter nights have revealed it to be a very different-looking ginger cat: bushy tailed, long, sleek and foxy. I'm still waiting for my garden's first actual fox, but I suppose, in the meantime, this fellow will do. I haven't found out if the bushy-tailed cat eats vomit, though, as he hasn't let me close enough to ask him, and I sense he is even more unlikely to since, in an uncharacteristic territorial gesture the other evening, The Bear frightened him off with one of his best 'gargling with lighter fluid' noises.

What with the bushy-tailed cat's mournful meowing and Ralph loudly talking about himself in the third person, the house remains a hive of cat activity around dawn. Gemma can sleep through this stuff, but I know from experience that it's no use for me to try to. If I get back to the land of nod after Shipley has shouldered open the bedroom door and attacked me with a machine-gun fusillade of expletives at 4.30 a.m., I'll only wake up again half an hour later, when Alan lands heavily on the conservatory roof.

Last weekend, I told Deborah about Alan's early-hours landings, and she seemed surprised.

'But we keep Alan in every night. It couldn't have been him.'

'But I saw him this morning. He looked right at me.'

'What time was this?'

'Probably about five. Maybe twenty past.'

'No, it couldn't have been Alan. We never let him out until about seven.'

'Will you be keeping him in tomorrow until about that time?'

'Definitely.'

The next morning, upon hearing the thump on the roof at about 5.30 a.m., I rushed to the window. As I did so, I saw a moonlike ginger face turn and stare back at me, in apparent hurt. The two of us froze in our positions for ten seconds, then he was gone. He looked well, I thought. There was still a softness about his face. As ever with Graham, I had so many questions. Where had he been all this time? Had he tried a new neighbourhood, got tired of it and decided that we weren't so bad after all? Maybe he had never been away, and had been lurking in the dark spots around the house all the time? Maybe it wasn't Graham at all, but yet another lookalike: the latest produce of the nest of feral ginger cats that seemed to reside somewhere in the neighbourhood? Whatever the case, I felt – though perhaps I was deluding myself – that I'd seen just a flicker of hope in that face as it stared back at me.

What we're looking at here is a long shot, admittedly. That was four days ago, and I haven't seen Graham since. The current market is not an easy one to sell a house in, but if all goes to plan we could be out of here in as little as three months. That's a relatively short time in which to win back the modicum of trust a feral cat ever had in you, and make him feel at home in your company.

A feral cat, that is, whose balls you cut off without asking. But I'm not ruling anything out.

I've been in a similar position before, of course: that of being on the verge of a house move and not knowing whether or not a cat would end up joining me for it. As I prepared to move from London to Norfolk in the autumn of 2001, The Bear had gone on an epic, pivotal six-week wander, and only returned in the nick of time. Dee and I didn't take many photos of him during that period – this being a time before cameraphones and the corporate merger that meant cats got to be in charge of the Internet – but I recently found a couple of the rare ones that we did take and was reminded again of what a tightly wound, wilful cat he'd been back then: of how, on the night he'd run away, he'd forced his then-much-wirier body through a sash window that had been opened no more than a crack; of how, on the day he'd come back, he'd run, for the first time ever, into my arms and clung to me so hard, and – even though he'd smelled of cabbage and dead things – I'd held on just as tightly.

I speculated to my dad recently on the phone about just how different both my life and The Bear's might have been, had he not returned home in time to join me and Dee in Norfolk, but he was having none of it.

'ALL OF THIS WAS ALWAYS GOING TO HAPPEN,' he said. 'IT WAS PLANNED OUT LONG AGO. IF YOU THINK OTHERWISE YOU'RE JUST KIDDING YOURSELF. DO YOU GET CHAVS IN JAPAN?'

'But what about the frog in your shoe?' I replied. After

their Christmas together, the new toad had left my dad's running shoe. Not long afterwards, a frog had moved into the gardening shoe favoured by the original toad. 'What if the toad had never come to my house, or if we hadn't realised it, and you had taken it back home with you? It might still be living in the shoe. Then we would have never had this conversation. Or, if we had, it might have been slightly different, and lasted a different amount of time, which could have meant you were later going into town this afternoon, and you didn't, I dunno, say ... bump into an old friend, leading to a revelation about your past, which might have changed the rest of your life. Even me deciding to say "Onions!" right now could be changing both of our futures. Onions! All this tiny stuff is sending our lives in different directions all the time, and it's all down to the decisions we make.'

'YOU'RE TALKING CRAP. YOU DON'T UNDER-STAND HOW PREDESTINATION WORKS AT ALL. DID YOUR MUM TELL YOU THAT THE KITTEN HAD BEEN TO THE TIP AND THE SUPERMAR-KET WITH ME?'

'She did, yes. I'm glad he's OK.'

Floyd's latest habit is to sneak into any vehicle that happens to be standing anywhere in or around the twitchell near my mum and dad's house. This has led my dad to genuinely contemplate adding a second sign to the 'PLEASE DRIVE SLOWLY: CATS PLAYING IN TWITCHELL' one, reading 'PLEASE CHECK YOUR CAR OR VAN FOR ANY SIGN OF OUR CAT BEFORE YOU LEAVE THE AREA'. Vehicles Floyd has recently stowed away inside include my car, a Post Office van, and a Currys truck that was delivering a new TV to one of my mum and dad's neighbours. Fortunately, he's been discovered each time before the drivers have left, but last week, when my dad was loading some garden waste into the car and left the boot open, he snuck inside very quietly. He poked his head into the gap between the front seats about twenty minutes later, when my dad was already halfway to the supermarket, where he was due to get provisions for Roger and Bea, the nonagenarians next door, some of which they would no doubt later eat in the comfort of their greenhouse.

All this brought me back to a recurring vision I'd been having of my parents in three decades' time, at Roger and Bea's age, asking me to get their shopping for them, their house now completely overrun with animal life: the toads now not just in footwear in the porch, but happily taking their own seat at the dining table. The vision frightened me a bit, but perhaps not so much as it should have done.

'IF YOU'RE GOING OUT LATER, REMEMBER TO WOFFAL,' said my dad.

'Oh, are you saying that out loud as well now?' In the last few months, as a time-saving device, my dad had been writing 'WOFFAL' at the end of his emails to me: an acronym of his standard 'WATCH OUT FOR FOOK-WITS AND LOONIES' warning.

'YEAH. I'M GIVING IT A TRY AND SEEING HOW IT WORKS OUT. HAVE YOU GOT YOUR CAR READY FOR WINTER?'

'It's April the twenty-first.'

'I KNOW, BUT YOU CAN'T BE TOO CAREFUL. I'M NOT SURE I LIKE THIS NEW FROG THAT'S LIVING IN MY SHOE. IT'S A BIT MORE SNOOTY THAN THE TOAD.'

'Well, it might decide it doesn't want to be there any more, and you'll get a nice toad again instead. There's nothing you can do to change it. What will be will be. As you said, it was all decided a long time ago.'

'EXACTLY. YOU'RE LEARNING.'

As parental advice went, 'WATCH OUT FOR FOOKWITS AND LOONIES' had served me pretty well over the years. Of course, sometimes to really be able to watch out for the FOOKWITS AND LOONIES, you needed to have some experience in dealing with FOOKWITS AND LOONIES. I would never have had to tell a hardy perennial such as The Bear to WATCH OUT FOR FOOKWITS AND LOONIES, as no doubt he'd experienced plenty of them in his time (he had, after all, been living with Shipley for twelve and a half years). His eyes and those notches in his ears told a tale of plenty of FOOKWITS AND LOONIES. Yet those eyes also said, 'I have accepted the existence of these individuals and intend to be calm about it.' That and, as always, 'Can you tell me why I am a cat, please?'

I mentioned earlier that The Bear, as a cat, was not subject to the same natural, noticeable physical changes brought about in humans as a result of ageing, but that's not quite true. In looking at those photos of him from 2001, I noticed something which gave me a bit of a jolt: his eyes looked very different. Still sad, but less deep, and wide. And I realised it was true: that pained owl look of his had not quite been there back then. It was actually a result of time and experience.

'What is it, The Bear?' I, Gemma, and friends who visit the house will still ask, looking into those eyes. He'll answer only with another bereft look. While others shout and swear their way through the day, he continues to offer his silent commentary: all-knowing, wry, dignified, troubled.

Nowadays, at feeding time, Roscoe, Shipley and Ralph eat on the floor, but The Bear climbs onto the step stool above them. Partly because he is missing several teeth, he likes to go at his own sedate pace, carefully sucking the jelly off each chunk of mechanically recovered meat. As he does so, he will pause every fifteen seconds or so, as if paranoid an adversary might be creeping up behind him holding a Post-it note with the word 'Wanker' scrawled on it. He always gets his food first, and I stick around, making sure the others – OK, I'm primarily talking about Shipley here – don't muscle in on him. Some might say I'm spoiling him, but I see it as a fundamental part of the conditions I agreed to when I decided to live with my par-ticular set of cats. In a similar way, had you decided to take in as pets three salamanders and the art critic Brian Sewell, you'd find it necessary to segregate a little area purely for Sewell so he had space to work without being disturbed.

The Bear still has plenty of amazingly sprightly moments. He's struck up a quiet bond with Roscoe, who he has perhaps finally accepted as an ally, due to her continued, fearless baiting of Shipley. I've caved in and started allowing him in the bedroom again, and he and she often sleep on the bed together, their paws sometimes lightly brushing as she edges closer to him. A couple of weeks ago he could be witnessed jumping out at her, kittenishly, from behind her favourite mirror, no doubt in the process making her even more con-fused about that lookalike nemesis of hers who seems to live in it. He still plays shyly but enthusiastically with his old toy mouse, and the occasional deceased real one that Ralph and Shipley bring in and complacently discard. In the last few months, though, I've noticed the difficulty that The Bear has in climbing down from any object higher than his own head. The camp wobble to his walk is getting ever more wobbly and, when I stroke his back, it feels brittle, like Janet's did in his final couple of years. Over winter, he would sometimes shuffle towards the catflap, see that it was raining outside, then look up at me and turn around, as if to say, 'Oh, it's all a bit too much. I don't think I'll bother.' I've perhaps believed him, more than any of my other cats, to be invincible, purely because he's withstood so much, but I should probably prepare myself for the fact that The Bear might not keep going strong for another twenty-two years and become the world's oldest ever feline.

I try not to imagine life without The Bear, but when I let myself slip towards doing so, only a confused, blurry picture emerges. I find it easier to imagine myself with an entirely different name and career, living in a country I've never visited. I really do love all of my cats equally, and for different reasons, but my relationship with The Bear is unique: not so much a bond with a cat, but the kind of attachment you might have to a mute friend you'd met in a hostage situation, and who'd been burdened with the job of feeling every emotion twice as acutely as anyone else.

It's a shame there weren't more photos of him taken earlier in his life, but I take plenty now. People have a habit, in the age of cameraphones and social networking, of being a bit too quick to turn all sorts of experiences into a 'memory', but I know it will be important for me to remember The Bear. When he is gone (and it pains me even to write the word 'gone'), maybe I will finally crack, and go back on everything I've told myself about cat-related paraphernalia. Perhaps the photos will spread out across the walls of my next house, until there is barely any paintwork visible. Who knows? Perhaps I'll get a tattoo dedicated to him as well. He certainly deserves a tribute of some permanence, because he's been such a good friend, such an inspiration: a cat who's weathered the tough stuff in his life – the plastic bag he was dumped in, Shipley, Biscuit's rejection of his love, his several illnesses, the injuries inflicted by all those other, more violent cats alongside whom he just wanted to live in peace, his many house moves, the early uncertainty about which human would be his forever human – and never let it turn him bad, instead growing progressively nicer, more charismatic, more *him*, as a result.

Maybe he did go through a stage where he had the capacity to be a bit swaggering and indifferent, like my other cats, or maybe his eyes saw too much too soon for that to be possible, then just kept seeing more. I wonder, if he had his chance to do it all again, in a different way, whether he'd take it. Perhaps not. Yes, he might be younger, and scar-free. He could have the confidence to hurtle up a tree or rip a vole's face off. And that would be great for him in many ways. But what wisdom would he lose in the process? What

enigma, which layers? Would he be so warm and interesting to be around?

And – crucially – could you then still say that he was
truly The Bear?

Acknowledgements

A huge thank you to Hannah Boursnell, my editor, and the rest of the team at Little, Brown, who believed in this book from the word go, and fulfilled my wish for a cover that reflected its content – which, as I've realised in the past, is not always an easy thing to find in the world of twenty-first-century animal-themed non-fiction. I am also massively grateful to Trent McMinn for taking such a lovely shot of The Bear for the cover (and for being very forgiving when I threw turkey in his hair by mistake), and to the following people for their encouragement during the book's creation: my fantastic parents Jo and Mick Cox, Gemma Wright, Martin Fletcher, Kate Carter, Jazzmine Breary, Laura Penn, Pat Bristow, Adele Nozedar, Rebecca McMahon, Amy Corcoran, Hannah Harper, Jack Burton, Karen Nethercott, Ian Curtis, Will Twynham, Mary Epworth, Amy Lyall, Emily Aaronson, Elizabeth McCracken, Stephen Dray, Jonny Geller, Joe Hollick, Ed Wilson, Rebecca Willers, Emma Hope, my neighbours Deborah and David, and anyone who's ever sent me a nice message about my writing over the Internet.

If you enjoyed reading about The Bear, Ralph, Shipley and Roscoe, you can keep up-to-date with their antics in a variety of ways:

Twitter
The Bear: @MYSADCAT
Ralph: @MYSMUGCAT
Tom: @cox_tom
Use the hashtag #goodbadfurry to talk about the book.

Facebook
www.facebook.com/pages/Under-The-Paw/93407930986

Pinterest
www.pinterest.com/goodbadfurry/

Blog
www.littlecatdiaries.blogspot.co.uk
www.tomcoxblog.blogspot.co.uk

Tom's website
www.tom-cox.com